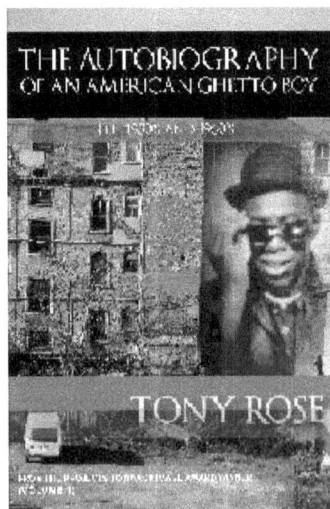

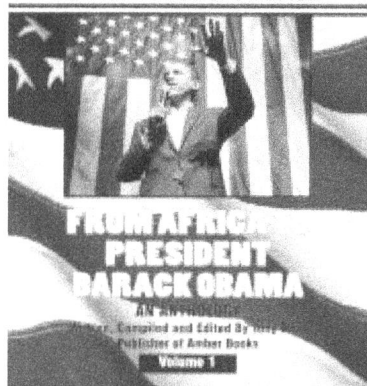

APPLAUSE FOR ROLAND BARKSDALE-HALL

"Your outstanding plenary presentation 'Healing Through Storytelling (Drum, Rap & Story)' was a major reason for the…Seventh National African American Student Leadership Conference's success. More than 1000 students from 162 different institutions and representing 37 different states were in attendance."

—A.J. Stovall, Ph.D., Conference Coordinator Seventh National African American Student Leadership Conference Chair Division of Social Studies, Rust College, Holly Springs, Mississippi

"Roland Barksdale-Hall is passionate about making a difference in the lives of young people…"

—Jacqueline Pitts, MA, author *The Children of Wasafa: A Message to Gang-Bangers*

His book Freedom Roads was a "wake-up call to all people… to face our greatest fears, get back to loving ourselves… and making our institutions more healthy."

—The Newsletter of the Black Caucus of the American Library Association

"Thank you for giving us a "Call to Action-with a plan!" Leadership Under Fire draws upon the work of our ancestors and elders and challenges us, as individuals and as a people, to look within ourselves and commit to the principle of collective work & responsibility to overcome the challenges we face as a family, a community and a nation".

Councilman Russel C. Neal, Jr. Akron City Council, Ward 4

"As a minister, counselor, writer, author, historian and poet, Brother Barksdale's dynamic voice and balanced scholarship is a powerful testament… His compelling research, fluid writing and activism are proof…He is an Imhotepian builder who has transcended modern time and space to journey down freedom roads".

—Anthony B. Mitchell, Sr., Ed.D., Instructor, Department of African American Studies, Penn State University Greater Allegheny

"In recognition of your important contribution to the ongoing fight against hatred and intolerance in America. And to honor your commitment to making a difference in your community. Thank you for taking a stand."

—Morris Dees, Founder, Southern Poverty Law Center

Barksdale's (1999) work, Healing is the Children's Bread and his current masterpiece, Leadership Under Fire, are must possessions (and study) for African American families. Both these groundbreaking works offer profound instruction, insights and powerful testaments to the courage, wisdom and spirit of our ancestors and generations of their descendants...
—Anthony B. Mitchell, Sr., Ed.D., Instructor, Department of African
American Studies, Penn State University Greater Allegheny

"Thus is the second year the Library has conducted a successful program for the youth in our community with the wonderful leadership of Mr. Roland Barksdale-Hall... The library opened its doors to over 50 people taking part in our African American History celebration... Participants enjoyed the sounds of African music, experienced the site of traditional African garb, learned about African American history through a scavenger hunt, and enjoyed a fantastic lunch..."
—Amy Jo Geisinger, Director,
Community Library of the Shenango Valley

"Congratulations... Such program delivery is so vital to the African American community. The presence which has been established... educates and frees the human spirit... Glad to see you are still passionate about history and genealogy. You are very deserving."
—Loretta O'Brien Parham, CEO and Director
Atlanta University Center Woodruff Library

"Fascinating how Roland Barksdale-Hall weaves leadership through his own experience, history and culture. A true 'diverse' voice of leadership."
—Marie Cini, Ph.D., Vice Provost and Dean,
School of Management and Technology at City University of Seattle

Roland Barksdale-Hall is an SBA truth-teller!...SBA truth-tellers reawaken our consciousness and guide us toward the path of spiritual healing, harmony and balance. Bro. Barksdale's service to community and tireless efforts to tell Sankofa stories epitomizes the highest qualities of our rich oral tradition.
—Anthony B. Mitchell, Sr., Ed.D., Instructor
Department of African American Studies, Penn State University
Greater Allegheny

Leadership Under Fire:

Advancing Progress,
Communicating, Teaching and
Setting Communities at Liberty

Leadership Under Fire:

Advancing Progress, Communicating, Teaching and Setting Communities at Liberty

Roland Barksdale-Hall

Amber Books
Phoenix <> Los Angeles <> New York

Leadership Under Fire:
Advancing Progress,
Communicating, Teaching and
Setting Communities at Liberty

Amber Books
1334 East Chandler Boulevard, Suite 5-D67
Phoenix, AZ 85048
e-mail: AMBERBK@aol.com
www.AmberBooks.com
www.TonyRoseEnterprises.com

Tony Rose, Publisher/Editorial Director
Yvonne Rose, Associate Publisher
The Printed Page, Layout/Design

Amber Books are available at special discounts for bulk purchases, sales promotions, fundraising or educational purposes. For details, contact: Special Sales Department, Amber Books, 1334 East Chandler Boulevard, Suite 5-D67, Phoenix, AZ 86048, USA.

Paperback ISBN #: 978-1-937269-56-2
Ebook ISBN # 978-1-937269-57-9
Library of Congress Control Number: 2016954223

"For the creation waits in eager expectation for the children of God to be revealed…the creation will be liberated from its bondage to decay and brought into freedom…"

Romans 8: 19, 21 (NIV paraphrase)

In Remembrance

To our beloved saints of the historic Emanuel African Methodist Episcopal Church in Charleston, South Carolina, who have gone home to their heavenly reward:

- The Rev. Clementa Pinckney, 41, Emanuel's pastor, father of two, South Carolina state senator;
- The Rev. Depayne Middleton Doctor, 49, ordained Baptist minister, mother of four;
- Cynthia Hurd, 54, librarian and county's housing authority board member;
- Susie Jackson, 87, a gospel singer along with her five sisters;
- Ethel Lance, 70, Emanuel's sexton, mother of five and the Galliard Center's custodian;
- Tywanza Sanders, 26, entrepreneur, motivational speaker and poet;
- The Rev. Daniel Simmons, 74, honorable U.S. Army veteran and counselor to disabled veterans;
- The Rev. Sharonda, 45, communicator par excellent, mother of three, speech pathologist, beloved high school track coach;
- The Rev. Myra Thompson, 59, teacher, guidance counselor.

They moved our hearts.

During the 170th Anniversary Celebration of Metropolitan African Methodist Episcopal (A.M.E.) Church, Washington, DC, (l-r) Bishop Vinton Randolph Anderson Presiding Prelate Second Episcopal District, A.M.E. Church; Rufus Tiefing Stevenson; The Reverend Dr. Louis-Charles Harvey, then Pastor Metropolitan AME Church, Washington, DC stand in front of portrait of The Reverend Richard Allen, a social activist and founding father of the African Methodist Episcopal Church.

Dedication

To The Rev Richard Allen, Clergy, Members of the A.M.E. Church and Rufus Tiefing Stevenson, and all those who struggled and endured and to future generations of free people to follow.

Dear Soldiers, Friends, Sons, Daughters and Sibs,

On Memorial Day Weekend we were blessed to attend and worship the Lord with Rufus Tiefing Stevenson at Metropolitan African Methodist Episcopal (A.M.E.) Church in Washington, D.C. The Rev. Dr. Ronald E. Braxton, pastor of Metropolitan A.M.E., shared a powerful message, entitled "The Courage to Stand Tall and Live." The text was taken from Romans 5:1-5, in referencing the suffering of Apostle Paul.

The points we took home included: 1) In Jesus Christ we can become all he wants us to be. We can get it together with God; 2) With courage we can stand in the face of obstacles. We can boast in God even when we are hemmed in; 3) If we take courage in the Lord, God will not disappoint us. Something critical for us we can hold on to through life: In Jesus Christ we can stand tall and live.

Peace be unto you,
Roland Barksdale-Hall

Acknowledgments

Each one reach one, each one teach one.

I would like to thank God for a vision and special people. Tony Rose, Publisher/CEO of Amber Communications Group, Inc., for creating a positive space for home folk to discuss community empowerment and Yvonne Rose, the best editor in the world. Members of Charleston's Emanuel African Methodist Episcopal Church for a powerful message of love and forgiveness. Eufaula's Emmanuel African Methodist Episcopal Church for roots and wings. National Association for the Advancement of Colored People for courage and knowledge of our past struggle to press on. BCALA leadership (Gladys, Stanton, Bobby, Sekou, Wanda) for my experience at the *BCALA News*. Tamela Tenpenny-Lewis for writing the foreword and an offer to serve as the Afro-American Historical and Genealogical Society Director of Publications. Max Rodriguez, founder of the Harlem Book Fair, who shared a venue at the Schomburg's Langston Hughes Auditorium and for my service as Managing Editor of *QBR The Black Book Review*. Penn State University and the Association of Research Libraries' Office of Management Studies for leadership training in Denver, Colorado. Larry C. Pickett, Sharon Flake and Jacqueline Pitts for sharing their passion. Youngstown State University, Victor Wantatah and Keith J. Lepak for wisdom shared, an office to write this manuscript, as well as an invitation to teach in the Africana Studies Department. John Lima, publisher, and James Raykie, Jr., editor of *The Herald*, who first published my leadership column. Linda and M. Mike McNair, co-publishers of *The Buckeye Review*, who published my community column. My advisor Dr. Marie Cini and the faculty at Duquesne University of the Holy Ghost for their leadership and guidance. Denice Dennison, Andrea Lovelace, Larry C. Pickett, Winfred V. Torbert and Erroline Williams, who enrolled along with me in the first leadership class for leadership perspectives. Northwest Pennsylvania Rural AIDS Alliance for a grant to attend the National Association of Black Storytellers Conference. Olympio Vormawor for encouraging publication of my speeches. Nannette Livadas, Holly Campbell and Sheila White for encouragement and a positive environment. Clarion University of Pennsylvania for a faculty development grant to attend the Seventh National African American Student Leadership Conference, Rust College, Holly Springs, Mississippi, held January 12-13, 2001 where I organized a plenary session, "Healing Through Storytelling (Drum, Rap, and Story)." Mentors, who I have been graced with in my life and provided inspiration, include Alexander and Martha Cromartie, David Myers, Gladys Smiley Bell, Dr. Stanton F. Biddle, Jeff Curtis, Kate Curtis, Drynda Johnston, Dr. E. J. Josey, Sylvia Cooke Martin, Gloria Reaves, Rufus Tiefing Stevenson, Loretta O'Brien Parham, Salvador B. Waller and Barbara Williams. My students again and again have provided fresh new insights. Faithful supporters of this project included Drusilla and Imanuel-Tiefing Barksdale-Hall. I take full responsibility for any errors. Grace be unto you and peace.

—R. Barksdale-Hall

Contents

Mr. Barksdale-Hall with his 2013 Afro-American Historical and Genealogical Society Distinguished Service Award and American Society of Freedman Descendants Senior Fellow Medal in the Quinby Street Resource Center Library.

Foreword

I have known Roland Barksdale-Hall since 1998. As an indirect witness of his skill set I would label Roland as a narrator of African American history, an obedient messenger of the ancestors and one to exhibit a positive impact to ensure success, growth and well-being of the Afro-American Historical & Genealogical Society, Inc.

Upon my election as National President in 2012, I instinctively knew that appointing Roland as Director of Publications would provide a profound impact on the distribution of records and repositories, DNA and genetics research, migration paths, writing and publishing family history, and family history research among other professional topics to our more than 1200 members, 30 chapters across the United States and those interested in the African Diaspora.

From the onset, Roland formalized his goals for AAHGS by making recommendations, assuming overall responsibility for publications (e.g. *AAHGS Journal, AAHGS Newsletter*, other print publications); and has ensured continuous publication. Before his appointment in the latter part of 2012 we were four journals behind in publication. Since that time, Roland has through immeasurable contributions and personal sacrifice brought us current by publishing three double issues of the journal, more than 16 issues of the newsletter, an impending journal and the production of *A Written History of the Afro-American Historical & Genealogical Society, Inc. 1977 – 2014*.

It was indeed an honor for me as National President to bestow upon Roland Barksdale-Hall the AAHGS President's Award presented to a member who has rendered outstanding service to AAHGS for a minimum of five (5) years at a personal sacrifice of time of which the President alone is the sole selector of the recipient of this award. In addition, the National Awards Committee honored Roland with the Distinguished National Service Award, presented to an individual who has rendered extraordinary, dedicated service of direct benefit to the AAHGS organization at the national level. Such service may be for a single act or for continuing service which far exceeds expectations in support of AAHGS national leadership in achieving the goals of the AAHGS organization. Only members of AAHGS are eligible for this award.

These are but a few, but not limited to the acts of leadership displayed by this committed individual that has directed his vision into reality by raising the performance of our publications to a higher standard. His leadership is defined by his results and for that, I am grateful!

Tamela Tenpenny-Lewis
AAHGS National President (2012-2015)

Introduction

Leadership Under Fire: Advancing, Communicating, Teaching and Setting Communities at Liberty is our story of personal transformation. It also is a call to reignite our dreams, reexamine our journey to freedom, rebuild our communities and reclaim our backyards. *Leadership Under Fire* pushes us to acknowledge a changing world, break with self-destructive patterns and assume our rightful place as global leaders. A leader acts under fire. The work is divided into four parts to form the acrostic ACTS: Part I *Advancing* progress; Part II *Communicating* in tough times; Part III *Teaching* ancestors and counter-narrative history; Part IV *Setting* communities at liberty. We discuss what emotional landmines exist in the real world, share lessons from the classroom, on the streets, within the church and in the ghettoes and public housing communities.

Leadership Under Fire expressly is written to address leadership development among the hurt and dispossessed communities of the globe, in particular the African Diaspora. From the classroom we examine best teaching practices, the pioneering works of Chinua Achebe to see what leadership looked like in the past and what lessons can be drawn to present times. Chinua Achebe's classic, *Things Fall Apart, No Longer At Ease* and *Anthills On The Savannah* should be required reading, despite humanities course offerings in leadership focus upon western civilization.

We share personal reflections on leadership development. The biography revisits the leadership journey of up until recent, an unsung hero, teacher-librarian, community activist and ordained minister and author. *Leadership Under Fire: Advancing, Communicating, Teaching and Setting Communities at Liberty represents* the fruition of leadership development at Duquesne University, Pittsburgh, Pennsylvania, titled *Children of Promise in the House,* resulted in his graduation with a Master of Leadership and Liberal Studies in August 2000. We later published *Freedom Roads, The Transformation* (Barksdale-Hall Educational Services and Training, 2003). Throughout the program of studies at Duquesne University we reflected upon and sought insights into the intersection between our leadership learnings and the African American community.

Leadership Under Fire is the third work in an introspective trilogy, speaks to the real deal in our communities and the critical leadership piece. *Healing is the Children's Bread: Complete with the Holistic Health Guide* by (Barksdale-Hall Educational Services and Training, 1999) the first work started off the series and addresses our individual and collective need for healing. *The African-American Family's Guide to Tracing Our Roots, Healing, Understanding and Restoring Our Families* (Amber Books 2005) speaks to our genuine experience and healing of families. *Leadership Under Fire* is one-part personal leadership odyssey, another part of a guide for everyday people.

We look at what can help us to stay grounded and how we can go back to liberate others in our faltering communities, offer preparation for moving out, and touching those who are wounded and hurting in our communities. We hear perspectives from authors, publishers and grassroots leadership in our communities. The book offers a twelve-step plan to take our communities back.

- Do your homework, know the facts and real deal in our community;

- Keep an open pipeline to the media;

- Know the who, what, where, when and how of government and community action agencies;

- Take ownership of the problem, know the history and project future implications;

- Get on the agenda, find out how much time you have, prepare a presentation that meets the deadline;

- Identify your contribution to solving the problem; remember you represent your constituent's interests;

- Bring all the stakeholders to the table, take notes and prepare to listen to all views;

- Identify resources, action plan, tasks, deadlines and responsible parties;

- Schedule follow up meetings, call with reminders before the meeting;

- Make it your business to check up on completion of tasks and follow up with responsible parties

- Chart future plans, Acknowledge the contributions of all parties

- Build and maintain healthy relationships; keep the lines of communication open.

Leadership Under Fire offers solutions. Life experience has been the cocoon where his metamorphosis taken form and crystallized. The metamorphosis began with a passion. A self-help study guide asks tough question to evoke constructive thought and discussion. There are no right answers or wrong ones, though we respectfully call for thoughtful consideration. Our insights, which occur as we read, can be stored in "Our Great Ideas Notebook," which simply can be a plain notebook with lines or a blank journal for later reflection or group discussion. The book offers one hundred ways to lead.

The book offers twelve tools to meet 21st century challenges.

- Laugh, enjoy life and celebrate the rich African American culture,

- Eat right, exercise and watch your blood pressure,

- Vote in local, state, and national elections,

- Find solutions through civic engagement, partner government and community,

- Read, rap with an elder and instill positive values,

- Network and collaborate, get our dollars to work,

- Commit to a project, hone leadership skillset and excel in what we do,

- Take a calculated risk, pursue our passion, birth a vision, then pass the baton, become a mentor,

- Join the NAACP, support the Urban League and social justice organizations,

- Study genealogy and history, visit museums and rethink our past,

- Join a Black Caucus, support a Black business and technological space,

- Let's all pull together, take responsibility for ourselves and our communities.

Leadership Under Fire: Advancing, Communicating, Teaching and Setting Communities at Liberty salutes the noble efforts of our enslaved ancestors. Free-born persons later sought to build a viable church, sacred and secular communities. Inventors, dreamers and achievers helped to build America and opened wide the freedom floodgates. *Leadership Under Fire* offers a clarion call to get back to loving ourselves and one another.

—Roland Barksdale-Hall

PART I
Advancing Progress

Chapter One
Advancing Ground

Are We There Yet?

I gave "Advancing Ground, Are We There Yet?" as the opening presentation, then entitled "Lest We Forget," at the "Black? Male? Struggling? Forum," held at Ruth A.M.E. Zion Church, Sharon, Pennsylvania. The message later ran as a two-installment series, titled "Black Male Progress: Are We There Yet?" in the AAHGS News.

rides

raccoon-face engine draws Americana
inside
the shadows of separate but equal
etch themselves in my body's slumber
black-face porters mime errand boys
staunch belly-heavy conductors
like old military men in starched blues
haunt corridors
at another time the ummmmmmmmmmmmhhh
of the Dixie flyer carried
coffee people, shoe box lunches
chickens (both alive and fried)
    miles mo' on elastic bumble seats

    packed in Jim Crow cars
unable to relieve themselves
bushes blot fo' Birmingham gals' sleep:

suddenly I am awakened
"Are we there yet?"
"Pittsburgh," comes my station call
"you're from the Hill."
from my mind's fog I return
    "no… Oakland."
    "oh!" the pale-face conductor belches
    "but that's a nice section of town!"
    "why bother," I sigh:
    movin' toilets ain't easy you know.

I am humbled to be at the altar where Pops moaned and prayed. "Do you want these books?" My father sat at the kitchen table and pointed to a Crisis *Magazine*. Pops sowed a "gift from the heart" and purchased the multi-volume set of Black history and literature books. Pops and the NAACP can be credited with cultivating my interest in African American history.

In the twenty-first century great strides have been made. In 2016, the eagerly anticipated and agitated for Smithsonian Museum of African American History and Culture opened on the National Mall in Washington, D.C. To imagine that someone by the name of Barack Hussein Obama would be elected the first African American president would have been unfathomable to prior generations, given the long shadow of inequality and social exclusion our ancestors faced in America. Today, with President Barack Obama in the White House it seems hard to imagine Washington, D.C. once was a "segregated town."

Yet, at one time our nation's capital indeed was segregated, in word and deed. The best-selling autobiography of Solomon Northrup's *Twelve Years A Slave* poignantly points out. You heard me right, Washington DC. once was a "segregated town." "Ain't that a turn-about!" Some might say, "Look the brothaman faces disrespect." Well, if you would hold your point for a second, we'll be getting to the issue in a moment. Right now, let's focus on how far we've come on the journey.

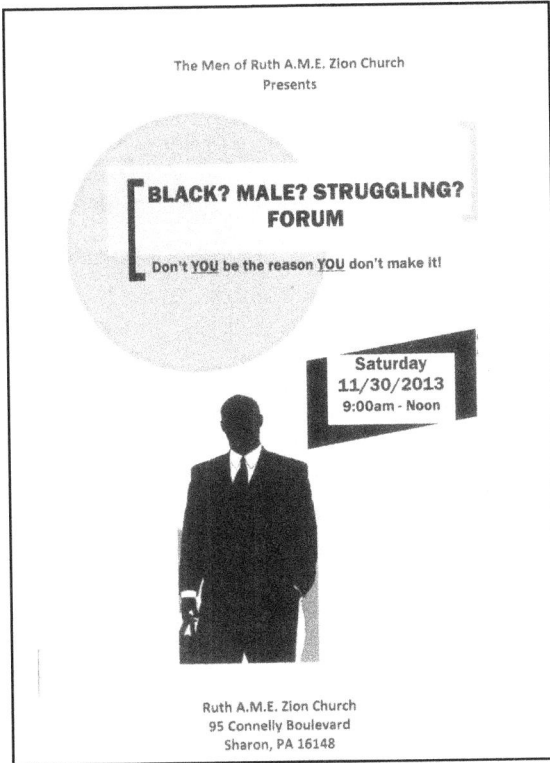

The Men of Ruth A.M.E. Zion Church
Presents

BLACK? MALE? STRUGGLING?
FORUM

Don't YOU be the reason YOU don't make it!

Saturday
11/30/2013
9:00am - Noon

Ruth A.M.E. Zion Church
95 Connelly Boulevard
Sharon, PA 16148

Black Male Forum program

Several years ago, President Obama gave a moving keynote address at the dedication of the Martin Luther King, Jr. Memorial located near the National Mall. Obama gratefully acknowledged the connection between the Civil Rights Movement and his political ascendancy. He rose from Senator of Illinois to become President of the United States. The dawn of the twenty-first century witnessed fruition to a two-decade long project of Alpha Phi Alpha Fraternity, Inc. the first African American fraternity, founded at Cornell University almost a century earlier in 1906. The brothers of Alpha Phi Alpha spearheaded a successful campaign drive to raise almost 120 million dollars for the colossal King Memorial. For sure, these have been momentous times we now live.

Dr. King spoke of having been to the Mountaintop and looked over into the Promise Land. *Are we there yet?* Ice Cube appears in a popular movie by that same name where he travels with two youth on a journey. The youth periodically ask, *"Are we there yet?"* This question calls us to explore our path to freedom. Let's take a few minutes to explore that question—*Are we there yet?*

So many of my college students at Youngstown State University, where I teach an undergraduate course "Introduction to Africana Studies: Artistic and Literary Perspectives," had heard of Dr. Martin Luther King, Rosa Parks, and Malcolm X. Yet, they never had heard of the Little Rock Nine and Daisy Bates. My students have asked, *"Why have we never heard of this before?"* They were not aware of outspoken individuals like Maria Stewart, Ida Barnet Wells, Henry Highland Garnett, David Walker, Martin Delany and John Brown, to name a few. Those in power teach the history of their group. The glaring lack of a historical consciousness among younger Americans, in particularly African Americans, Latinos, Native American, females, and economically disadvantaged whites, needs to be addressed in public schools.

At the Pittsburgh Afro-American Historical and Genealogical Society program author gave a flower talk about the Society's 1994 Women's History Month Honoree, Dr. Edna McKenzie (center) for her noble work, Freedom in the Midst of a Slave Society: A Documentary Supplement for Courses in the Afro-American Experience. Dr. Huberta Jackson-Lowman, co-director of the University of Pittsburgh Institute for the Black Family, looks on;

BLACK FAMILY

TRACE YOUR ROOTS DURING WOMENS HISTORY MONTH	*SEARCHING HISTORY AND REGAINING EMPOWERMENT*

The Institute For The Black Family

and

The Western Pennsylvania African American Historical and Genealogical Society
Present

The Third
Black Family History Forum

Saturday , March 12, 1994

The Henry Clay Frick Fine Arts Auditorium
University of Pittsburgh · Pittsburgh , PA 15260

Institute For The Black Family
University of Pittsburgh

Third Black Family History Forum program

How Was There Freedom in the Midst of a Slave Society?

My friend and mentor, Dr. Edna Chappell McKenzie, a Pittsburgh native, venerable national board member of the Association for the Study of African American Life and History and author of *Freedom in the Midst of a Slave Society: A Documentary Supplement for Courses in the Afro-American Experience*, stated "The Founders of the Created a Less-Than-Perfect Constitution."4 Section 2 of Article I of the United States Constitution (see paragraph three, the first sentence) contains what has become known as the "three-fifths" compromise. African-Americans were classified as three-fifths of a white man ("free persons"). Section 9 of Article

I (see paragraph one, first sentence) provided for the continuance of the slave trade for another twenty years to the year 1808.

Forms of resistance to slavery included: 1) Slave narratives, including the *Autobiography of Olaudah Equiano* to *Incidents in the Life of Harriet Jacobs*; 2) runaway; 3) work slow-downs 4) rebellions, including Nat Turner, Gabriel Prosser, John Brown; 5) abolition; 6) emigration.

An effect of the Revolutionary War was a momentary pricking of America's conscience. In some Northern States slavery was abolished. Vermont led the way in the abolishment of slavery. However, it made it hard for free Blacks to live in their state. Also laws were passed making it impossible for Blacks to own property. So the intent in Vermont was to entirely remove their state of Blacks. In Pennsylvania there was the 1780 Gradual Abolishment of Slavery.

Free Blacks in the North faced Black Codes and social exclusion. Social commentators have noted Sunday morning to be the most segregated time in America. At one time blacks and whites attended church together. Free Blacks were forced to worship in colored galleries in white churches. A person praying was interrupted and told to return to the gallery; such incidents at these churches led to the formation of the African Methodist Episcopal (A.M.E.) Church by the Reverend Richard Allen. The A.M.E. Zion Church, known as the Freedom Church, produced leaders. David Walker in his widely circulated publication, *David Walker's Appeal*, warned that the persistent mistreatment of enslaved individuals would lead to bloodshed. Free Blacks were kidnapped and sold into slavery. These flaws would precipitate a bloody Civil War. Additions to the U.S. Constitution later would be required.

- 13th Amendment passed by Congress on January 31, 1865, ratified on December 6, 1865, abolished slavery in the United States. *Are we there yet?*

- 14th Amendment ratified on July 9, 1868 made granted citizenship. *Are we there yet?*

- 15th Amendment ratified on February 3, 1870 provided black male citizens, excluding females, the right to vote. In 2013, Pennsylvanians—some minorities and poor voters—are challenged by a voter id law with potential to disenfranchise them. *Are we there yet?*

The era of sharecropping became slavery by another name. With the promise of "Forty Acres and a Mule" being fleeting there was no way for African Americans to challenge the unfair business practices of unscrupulous white landowners. Still, seventy or more so years of terrorism, also known as lynching followed. The legacy of slavery was painstaking.

Author and Dr. Martha Bruce appeared in the Youngstown Vindicator doing a rendition of poem "W.E.B. and Booker T." by Dudley Randall for African American Read in for Youngstown Public Schools. Mayor Jay Williams read a speech by then Illinois Senator Barack Obama. The 2011 theme was "Voices of Hope and Courage."

Strategies to progress in freedom varied. Booker T. Washington promoted farming and skill development, avoiding politics at Tuskegee Institute. Ida B. Wells-Barnett promoted black self-help, suing and defending oneself with a gun—what we might know today as stand your ground; which was considered radical at a time when people gathered outside your door with a noose. The 1921 destruction of Greenwood District of Tulsa, where whites dropped bombs from planes went without compensation and recognition of the public wrong for the death and destruction of property for over sixty years.

Participation in military service was another strategy. The contributions of African Americans in the military are documented from the Revolutionary War to the present. African Americans have served in every conflict from the beginning. Still, in some circles a myth existed that African Americans were considered dumb and stupid: African Americans presumably were unable to fly a plane. *"Can you take me up there?"* Eleanor Roosevelt pointed to the sky and asked. The Secret Service Agents were unable to stop the First Lady. The African American pilot took her up and brought the First Lady safely back. During World War II the famed Tuskegee Airmen did not lose a plane that that they were protecting. The military was segregated up until World War II. In 1948, President Harry S. Truman desegregated the military through signing Executive Order 9981. *Are we there yet?*

Beginning in World War I running through World War II, the mass migration of African Americans from rural southern reaches to industrial urban centers occurred. One southern newspaper said it was not the "riffraff" leaving. Our ancestors were not complacent. Yet they moved in search of opportunity. Their movement contributed to the growth of Black Chicago, Philadelphia, Pittsburgh and Detroit.

Change has been an evolving process. Our ancestors agitated for better living conditions. Some died for the right to vote, as late as the 1950s. Children died in the 16th Street Baptist Church bombing in Birmingham. In recent times, progress is evident. Yet, there still remains room for change. As earlier mentioned, we can ill afford to think that the Founding Fathers were perfect for it denies the reality that they "Created a Less-Than-Perfect-Constitution." If it was still operating the same, many minorities and women would not be voting. The Trayvon Martin case was an indicator that just because something is legal does not mean that it is not an ethical dilemma. *"So are we there yet?"* you ask.

As earlier mentioned, we watched our hearts filled with joy the rise of Barack Obama from senator of Illinois to president of the United States. Yes, President Obama has faced challenges yet struggle goes with the territory. The point being Barack Obama is the President of the United States of America and the political process has worked in regard to the struggle for voting rights. Interracial cooperation was the best strategy to produce lasting social progress and continues to be. Before the Civil War there were white abolitionists, as well as black abolitionists at work. Realize the quest for freedom always has been a dynamic process and there will continue to be struggle. In the final analysis the1857 proclamation made by the great liberator, Frederick Douglass still stands today, *"Where there is no struggle, there is no progress."*

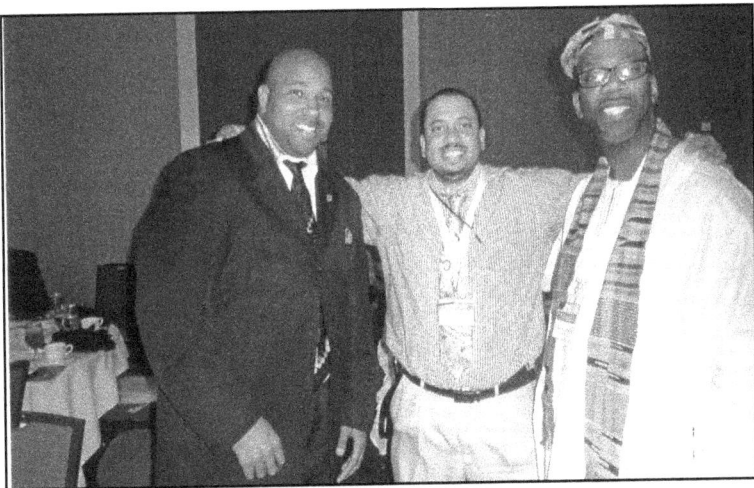

The author with the executive director of the Solomon Northup Foundation Clayton J. Adams (center), the Great-Great-Great-Grandson of Solomon Northup and teacher Mr. Scott at Afro-American Historical and Genealogical Society Awards Banquet in Pittsburgh, Pennsylvania.

How Can We Keep Our Ancestor's Memories Alive?

A few things we can do to celebrate our ancestors:

- Keep the memories of our ancestors' stories of resiliency (the ability to come back from setbacks) alive through storytelling; Join the Association for the Study of African American Life and History;

- Join the Afro-American Historical and Genealogical Society;

- Inquire with school board directors about course offerings at your local schools about the African American experience, minorities and women's history in your communities;

- Go see a cultural movie, such as the film based upon the autobiographical book by the same name *12 Years a Slave*.

Are we there yet? Well today you will have ample opportunities to inch closer pressing to the mark of being there. So I hold the utmost respect for our community activist, now President Barack Obama. Finally, let's keep our eyes on the prize!

The question of the day was a familiar one to me and Pops. As a boy I would ask. "Are we there yet?" Pops regularly packed up the Oldsmobile; Momma fried the chicken as we set off on our road trip from Pittsburgh west to Cincinnati through Kentucky. There were cities with names like Lexington that sounded like they stepped right out of the Revolutionary War.

I anticipated what was at the end of our road trip. Our trek carried us from the Steeler Nation to Big Foot Country. Pops came of age when we was colored in Alabama. Belonged to a warm and loving extended family. Kinfolk was so happy to see us come from "Up the Country." Made a big fuss over us, yes they did.

Big Momma who cooked meals for many a hungry niece and nephew, would ring a chicken's neck. Uncle Sam and Aunt Martha treated you royal. Would ask to keep us just a little longer. Uncle Lawrence would give us a box of peanuts. Aunt Troy would cook southern dishes. Aunt Dolly would give you a watermelon.

Well last summer we packed up the Toyota and took our family on a trek through the South. Visited Tuskegee University, home of the Tuskegee Airmen and checked out the George Washington Carver Museum. Under the direction of Colonel Benjamin O. Davis Jr., four squadrons of Black fighters had one of the best records of any Air Force fighter group. During World War II, the airmen earned 150 distinguished flying crosses. They flew 15,533 sorties, 1,578 combat missions, and never lost a bomber they escorted over North Africa and Europe! However, up until the mid-1990s, the Tuskegee Airmen, like the 92nd and 93rd Infantry Divisions, the 366th Infantry Regiment and the 761st Tank Battalion, were virtually ignored by mainstream America.

A Tuskegee resident, Michael Johnson, served up a delightful insider's tour replete with conversations with the elders. The town's good name unfortunately has been soiled by many when in fact the United States Public Health Service shoulders full responsibility for the infamous Syphilis Study. If you want the real scoop, read Harriet A. Washington's *Medical Apartheid: The Dark History of Medical Experimentation on Black Americans From Colonial Times to the Present* (Doubleday, 2006) and James H. Jones' classic *Bad Blood: The Tuskegee Syphilis Experiment* (Free Press, 1993). Took in the Civil Rights Memorial at the Southern Poverty Law Center in Montgomery. Paused for meditation at the granite wall with water rolling down over Dr. Martin Luther King's famous paraphrase of Amos 5:24— "Let justice roll down like waters and righteousness like a mighty stream." If you are unable to take your family on a historic trip through the South, read Christopher Paul Curtis's *The Watsons Go to Birmingham* (Delacorte 1995).

On the trip we snacked on finger-licking southern fried chicken. Laughed over saucy ribs and melt in your mouth banana pudding at Dreamland Bar-B-Q in Montgomery. Oh yes, the Barksdale kinfolk made a big fuss. "*By far the best part of the trip was time spent with family.*" Kids said.

"Are we there yet?" Kids still asked though. Laugh out loud! Some things don't change. Still talking about when we going back to our Dreamland. What do you got to do to reach your dreamland?

NOTES

Barksdale-Hall, "Black Male Progress: Are We There Yet?" *AAHGS News* (January/February 2015 and March/April 2015).

www.upcscavenger.com/wiki/martin_luther_king,_jr._ memorial/#page=wiki

Ploski, Harry A. and Roscoe C. Brown, Jr. The Negro Almanac. (New York: Bellwether Publishing, 1967).

McKenzie, Edna B. Selected Essays on Contemporary African American Issues (Verona, Pennsylvania: McKenzie Publications, 1998).

http://www.archives.gov

Life Applications

1. Are we free in today's society? Why or why not?

2. What does your American Dreamland look like? How do you plan to reach it?

3. What is the significance of the Black church to freedom in today's society?

Chapter Two
Prepare to Meet Your Dreams

Do You Know Where I Live?

Redeeming the discarded
He walks between the future
                    And the past.

He pauses pondering
He walks
Then pauses, pondering again.

His journey seems to be a dance
Celebrated among the hiddenly precious,

For even in the dimmest
Face
He seems to see the glimmer of
A gem.

D.L. Hall
My Barksdale Poem (1990)

Our dreams are dynamic and alive, transforming future generations' hearts, minds and souls. Grandma's presence, sometimes, can make all the difference in the world. As children, we recalled wonderful birthday visits to our Grandma's sanctuary. Some years before I was born, proceeds from the sale of my mother's family homestead for the neighboring Mesabi Street Apartments public housing helped pay for future generations' college education.

During the sixties Grandma kept a tidy two-story house with a well-manicured lawn on an adjoining lot perched on a steep hill. It was an anchor in my life. She produced wonderful patchwork quilts, undisturbed by outside forces. A wire fence separated her from the world of the projects. Kids from the projects sometimes climbed over the fence into her world nonetheless. Grandma lived out her days on a remaining lot of the family homestead adjoining the projects.

Grandma's love and hope at times have provided the inspiration for us to press on under fire. We prepared to meet a dream when we became the library director at the public housing Quinby Street Resource Center. We did not know the rewarding, yet challenging experience awaiting. We returned to the real world.

Crazy Quilt

Birthday came
C R AZ Y QUI L T on the bed, lined with
throw-rug.
Purples of sister's frock, settling there;
I hear these patchessss:
Crying for me, telling corny jokes, saying
Hushshshsh BE STILL.
Papa's green flannel, removed from work-shirt must,
Pats me on the head.
Maroon and gold, brother's ugly plaid,
Snuck in, wrestles me to bed.
Orange criss-crosses, that's Momma's apple pie,
Topped with French vanilla borders
And laced coconut beneath:
Delights of saucer-filled eyes,
Coaxing, "sleeeeeeeeeeeeeep."

"Grandma's craft,"
Sister tells me;
Of course…,
Now I can see.
Homespun snowflakes,
Yessss that's Grandma,
Like rocky-road, turtles, praline,
Grandma whispers, "My Momma shows me how, with thread
To pluck lovely chords, dashes of homespun
To turn houses into homes, pieces of scrap,
Don't you, don't you, DON'T YOU throw away,
Gives them to me. I knows the way.

Leaning over
Good night kisses mixes of goooood things,
Servings of vanilla sandwich cremes,
Dips of Bruton Scotch snuff,
I hears the spittle's ting
Against Hills Brothers' shredded can,
Lilac (soap) fills the room.
Grandma's presence is
Acceptance on failure-ridden days.
I feels those hands, warming me,
Saying, "boy, dooooooooos yo best."

TOP: *Author presents on genealogy with (l-r) Sylvia Cooke Martin, and Dr. Agnes Kane Callum, also known as the "Three Musketeers," at the National Mall Black Family Reunion Celebration held on the National Mall. BELOW: At the request of longtime friend Dr. Agnes Kane Callum (seated wheelchair) the author (back row, standing far right) was the keynote speaker for the Afro-American Historical and Genealogical Chapter Agnes Kane Callum 25th Anniversary Banquet held at St. Francis Xavier Church, Baltimore, Maryland.*

*Mr. Barksdale-Hall received from Kelvin Watson, BCALA president, the
2015 BCALA National Leadership Award at the National Conference of
African American Librarians in St. Louis, Missouri.*

When I received the prestigious 2015 BCALA National
Leadership Award, it was a high point in my career. Before leaving
for St. Louis, Missouri I faced a crisis. There was a shooting outside
the Quinby Street Resource Center. It was on a Sunday afternoon.
Nearly 40 children gathered for a birthday party. Police said it was
"a miracle a child was not hit." Reflecting upon how the shooting
nearly blanketed my community in a catastrophic silence, void of
children's laughter, made me pause and ponder. A bullet riddled

van was parked nearby the Center. Yet, in the midst of storm I found hope in a Grandma's face.

String about Service to Residents in Public Housing

A string on a list captured the moment:

RE: Dear BCALA - Mr. Barksdale-Hall: [BCALA] Pittsburgh Courier

Mr. Barksdale-Hall is the foremost authority on the restoration of our African American families in the ghetto and projects in America. We are proud at Amber Books to be the publisher of his book, THE AFRICAN-AMERICAN FAMILY'S GUIDE TO TRACING OUR ROOTS: Healing, Understanding, & Restoring Our Families (ISBN# 0-9749779-7-7).

Congratulations, Mr. Barksdale-Hall on receiving the 2015 BCALA National Leadership Award.

All the best,

Tony Rose

Publisher/CEO

Amber Communications Group, Inc.

Dear BCALA family,

The 9th NCAAL was like a wonderful family reunion! See New Pittsburgh Courier article

Thanks again to all for the award and a wonderful time,

With Appreciation,

Roland Barksdale-Hall, Librarian, Black Caucus of the American Library Association (BCALA), Community Activist and Author of *The African American Family's Guide to Tracing Our Roots: Healing, Understanding and Restoring Our Families*

Roland Barksdale-Hall <barksdalehall@gmail.com>

Thank you for your kind words, Mr. Rose. Three years ago, when I became the library director at the public housing Quinby Street Resource Center, I did not know the rewarding experience it would be. There is a desperate need in the ghetto and projects in America. I know the children and adults need the services we provide at the center. Right before going to the NCAAL we had a shooting right outside the center near where 40 children were gathering for a birthday party. The shooting occurred at 6:00 p.m. on Sunday. One adult was hit. It really is a miracle a child was not hit. Words cannot express the stress felt by residents and me. I feel like the children deserve better. This week a neighborhood church purchased the kids in our neighborhood book bags and school supplies. The two suspected gunmen fortunately have been captured. By the way, the suspects did not even live in the projects. To be able to serve people in the ghetto and projects in America and do what you love makes the 2015 BCALA Leadership Award all the more special. Black Lives Matter in the ghetto and projects!

to me

I take my hat off to you, sir!

Pray no harm comes to you or to any of the children.

God bless!

Tezeta L.

Retired librarian

to me

My Brother,

Tulu ugo gi…. take a bow!

Udo diri gi…. peace be with you.

-uzo

to Tezeta

Tezeta, you blessed me today,

God has been my source. I spoke with a Grandma the day following the shooting. She shares something special with me: How her love for her grandchildren made her come outside again, despite spending the night weeping.

In this grandma's eyes I saw something beyond the tears—here was a determination to weather the storm. I, too, share her determination and faith.

Our love for the children is greater than any fear. I am encircled by children's love. I appreciate your prayers for me and the children. Please also remember the Grandmothers as well.

Brother Barksdale

◇ ◇ ◇

Journal Entry about Tense Times

I teach financial literacy skills to public housing residents. I tell about the rewarding experiences in my chapter, "Collaboration Fits the Bill for Best Practices in Programming to Public Housing Residents" in the anthology *Library's Role in Supporting Financial Literacy for Patrons* (Rowman & Littlefield, 2016). With so much going on I closely watched the comings and goings at the door. An entry in our journal captured the tense times:

Today, I was alone at the Center when I saw an African American male and female come to the door and disappeared. The female came in and got on Facebook. I said, "Excuse me you have to sign in."

"I got to go to the bathroom." A young brother in sportswear with tattoos rushed down the hall.

"What's coming next?" I wondered.

He soon returned.

"You got to sign in," the female told him. She proceeded to chat about someone's birthday, this and that, punctuated by. "Should we go to the hospital now?"

I looked into his face. There was gauze over what appeared to be a cut on his cheekbone and dreadlocks. "What's his story?" I pondered.

He looked like he just stepped straight up out of Boyz n the Hood. His phone then gave a blast of urban lyrics.

"Are you in town? A voice said."

"Uhm…"

"I'm taking something…?"

"I'm in the library; I can't talk."

"Well, I need to know."

"Okay Grandma, hamburger."

I nodded a sign of approval.

He got up and left. I smelled smoke when he returned.

He then sat at the computer and made a call.

"Can I have the financial aid officer?"

There was a pause.

"I need to know your school code."

The female got up and left.

"Did you find what you were looking for?" I asked the young male.

"Yes, I got my application into a school of trade."

"What do you plan to study?" I inquired.

"Automotive technician."

"Wish you all the best. That's a good field."

The learning lesson was you cannot always see a dream. This young person was preparing to meet his dream. Grandma's influence has a long reach in our communities.

Life Applications

1. When I shared the story about the youth with Boyz N the Hood appearance surprised friends thought the young man was going to try and sell me something or worse. Why do you think others did not view his image as a dream seeker?

2. How do you think African American youth are viewed in general by society?

3. Compare and contrast the positive and negative perceptions of African American youth. What might our youth do to increase the positive perceptions?

Chapter Three
Building America

*How Did Inventors, Dreamers and Achievers
Open Wide the Freedom Floodgate?*

In recent times, I returned to our college alma mater and received
the Blue Black and Gold Award from the University of Pittsburgh
African American Alumni Council. Our research findings and
publication on the first African American graduate of the University
of Pittsburgh William Hunter Dammond (1873-1956) corrected
the official University of Pittsburgh history. Mr. William Hunter
Dammond was a product of Pittsburgh's Hill District, excelled as
a civil engineer, professor and inventor. Up until that time John
Coverdale Gilmore was considered the first graduate.

When I first approached the University the editor of the *Pitt
Magazine* was not interested. I was not dismayed. I just became
more determined to correct the official University history. I reached
out to a few other members of the African American Alumni
Council, namely Madalyn Turner Dickerson and Stephanie
Johnson.

We discussed what might be the best strategy, arrived with a
plan and began the implementation. We agreed upon a presenta-
tion on William Hunter Dammond during the African American
Alumni Council Homecoming Week Banquet. Robert Hill, the
then new African American University of Pittsburgh Director of
Publications, was to receive an invitation to attend. Our plan went
off as clock work: Robert Hill attended and heard about William
Hunter Dammond for the first time. I was asked if Dammond
looked like a white person. I produced a photograph of William

Hunter Dammond's, transcript and other supporting documents. My research stood verified.

Pitt Campaign Chronicle with Mr. Barksdale-Hall featured as a "Dreamer and Achiever."

The empowering story, "Dreamers and Achievers," what was called a "double celebration" appeared above the fold on the front page of the *Pitt Campaign Chronicle*. We were moved by the "profile of William Hunter Dammond, the first African American graduate of the University of Pittsburgh, as researched and written by Roland Barksdale-Hall" along with our stories. You can find the story on websites from University of Pittsburgh, the School of Engineering, in a documentary about the Pitt African American presence and *Blue Gold and Black Magazine* to African American inventor websites. The published story about Dammond was a reprint from my book, *Healing is the Children's Bread*. Well, my story about William Hunter Dammond has gone viral!

Dreamers and achievers tend to think outside the box. Making connections to the transformative power of the arts, employment skills and self-actualization hold keys to economic empowerment and community revitalization. At least that is partly how Bill Strickland has changed lives in post-industrial Pittsburgh. He came of age in Pittsburgh's rough Manchester community, where he faced poverty and lacked a sense of purpose up until high school when a teacher introduced him to ceramics. For the last thirty years Strickland transformed lives through his unique brand of philosophy, promoting self-actualization now instituted at the Manchester Craftsmen's Guild and Bidwell Training Center. Program offerings ranging from culinary, pharmacy to technology and photography provided underprivileged folks with the skill set to land good-paying jobs. He established an impressive track record with diverse supporters.

His message reaped benefits. In 1996, he became the recipient of a prestigious MacArthur Fellowship "genius" grant; followed by the International Economic Development Council's Citizen Award in 2005; and then Goi Award for advancement of world peace and humanity in 2011. He plans to replicate centers around the globe, beginning with the Akko Center in northern Israel. Arabs and Jews will work together in the Akko Center. For more on the topic read The Hope Maker in *The Pitt Magazine*, fall 2015.

William Hunter Dammond, civic engineer, inventor and college professor, at a family wedding in Pittsburgh, Pennsylvania;

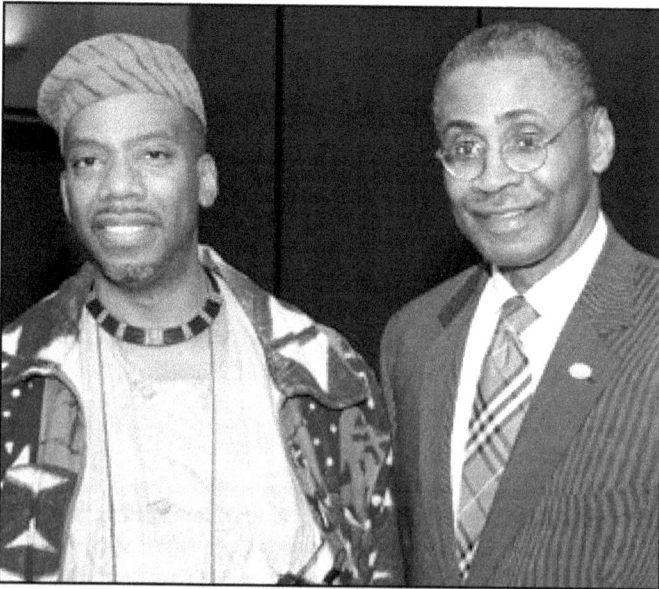

Author and Dr. Livingston Alexander, the first African American president at the University of Pittsburgh Bradford, following my keynote speaker for 2010 Black History Month Program.

No. 823,513

PATENTED JUNE 19, 1906.

W. H. DAMMOND.

SAFETY SYSTEM FOR OPERATING RAILROADS.

APPLICATION FILED FEB. 17, 1905.

2 SHEETS—SHEET 1.

WITNESSES

INVENTOR

William H. Dammond

By Fish & Thomas

Attorneys

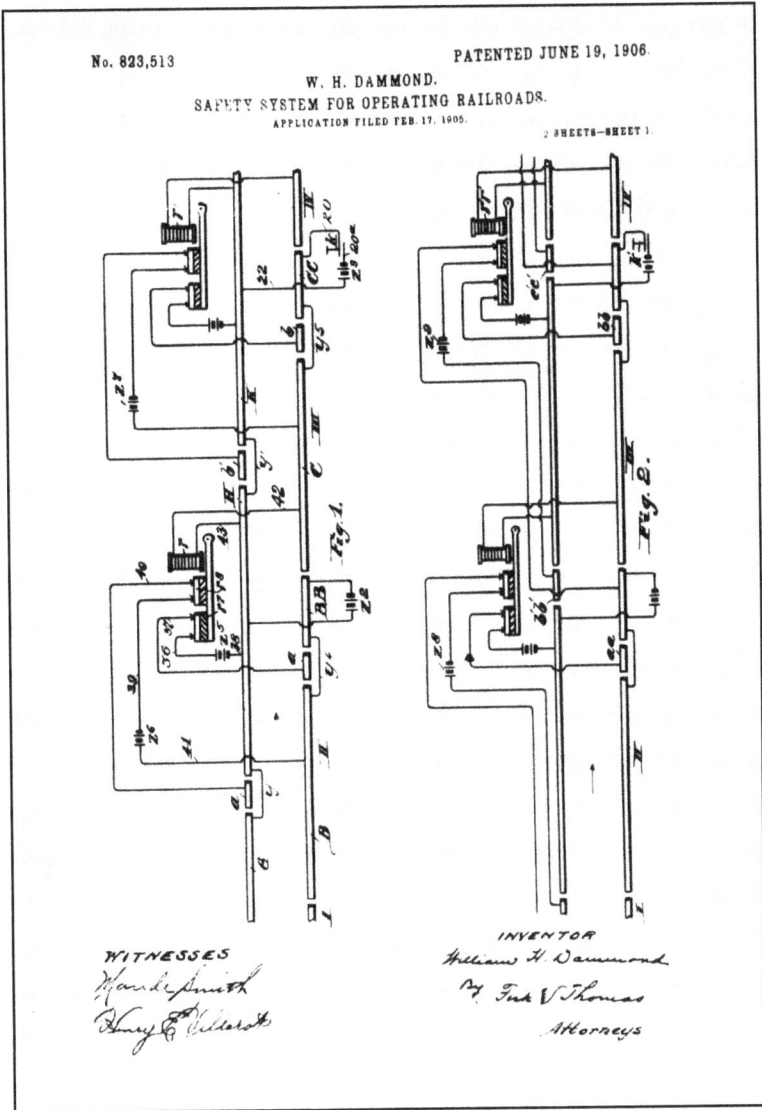

William Hunter Dammond's patent papers for a signaling circuit switch for railways.

*ABOVE: During Black History Month Mr. Barksdale-Hall was fea-
tured in the University of Pittsburgh Hillman Library exhibit showcase;
BELOW: Roland Barksdale-Hall received the Blue Black and Gold Award
at the University of Pittsburgh African American Alumni Council Brunch
and Special Black Greek and School Awards Presentation at the Pittsburgh
Hilton Hotel on October 25, 2009.*

Pitt LIS alumnus Roland Barksdale-Hall recognized as library expert

Roland Barksdale-Hall (MLS '84), the library director at the Quinby Street Resource Center, Sharon, PA, received the 2015 Black Caucus of the American Library Association (BCALA) National Leadership Award at the 9th National Conference of African American Librarians, held in August 2015. Barksdale-Hall received this honor in recognition of his significant and extraordinary contributions in service to the library profession in areas of leadership including scholarship, professional development, library education, and professional activities on the local or national level.

Barksdale-Hall serves as the Afro-American Historical and Genealogical Society (AAHGS) Director of Publications and was the recipient of the AAHGS James Dent Walker Award, the highest AAHGS award. He taught at the library school at Clarion University.

Barksdale-Hall is president and co-founder of JAH Kente International Inc., an organization that promotes the arts and genealogy throughout schools in metropolitan Washington D.C. area. He has served as the national youth director for Frontiers International, Inc. and as the vice president of the Buckeye Review and on the executive committee of the Black Caucus of the American Library Association.

Author was spotlighted in the Pitt School of Information Science's 2015 SIS E Magazine http://ischool.pitt.edu/news/index.php

Many of today's youth sadly remain unaware of my people's significant contributions to advancements in peace, science and technology. During Black History Month I developed a new African American History Day programming. Youth enjoyed African drumming and dancing. Components included a library display, trivia contest, scavenger hunt and Black History Month bingo.

Youth partnered with an adult mentor to look for inventions by African Americans posted throughout the public library. Images ranged from the traffic light and bicycle frame to the ironing board and lawnmower. New people visited and were registered for library cards. Program sponsors included the local public library and Frontiers International, an African American service organization.

In my backyard I found James Elmer Matthews (1873-1956), African American inventor, received a patent for a shearing guide, that clipped tin on August 22, 1916. He received no financial compensation for his invention that was used in the industry. He wrote a letter about how he received little, if any, compensation for his invention, which was used in tin plants. His patents included a safety lock and brake for sleds. From my research one historical commentator Hal Johnson concluded the "African American inventor toiled in obscurity while others benefited" (*The Herald*, March 15, 1998). Matthews became a staunch civil rights activist, who served as the first elected president of his local unit of the NAACP. He opened the door to equal employment opportunities in the mills. For more information on James Elmer Matthews read my book, African *American Inventive Genius: James Elmer Matthews (1886-1976) and William Hunter Dammond (1873-1956)* at the Smithsonian Institution Library.

Historian Henry "Skip" Louis Gates, Jr., Director of the W.E.B. Du Bois Institute for African and African American research at Harvard University, released the eight-volume *African American National Biography* (Oxford University Press 2008). Glad to be counted in the mix. In the classic *African American National Biography* more than four thousand entries of well-known figures like Doctor Martin Luther King to former Secretary State Colin Powell are found. I have an William Hunter Dammond entry in the *African American National Biography* on the Oxford African American Studies Center.

I researched a lesser known African American inventor, Andrew Jackson Beard for an entry in the *African American National Biography*. Andrew Jackson Beard (1849–1921), former slave and

Birmingham African American businessman, received a patent for his double plow on April 26, 1881; followed by a patent for the plow or cultivator on August 10, 1886. In 1889, Beard invented the rotary steam engine, which was promoted as being more efficient than conventional models at one tenth the cost and conserved twenty per cent of steam without risk of explosion. He received a patent for a significant safety-device, the automatic car-coupling on November 23, 1897. On a trek through the South I visited the African American inventor's hometown.

I stopped at Tuskegee University, checked out the accomplishments of George Washington Carver (1864-1943) and later got in research at the Birmingham Public Library's southern historical collection. George Washington Carver, African American agriculturalist, was widely known for his research on the peanut and crop rotation methods which changed the reliance on cotton as the major crop in the South. Popular tradition erroneously held that Carver never received a patent, because he presumably abstained from wealth and prestige. He received patents for three inventions: a cosmetic on January 6, 1925, followed by a process for producing paints on June 9, 1925 and another paint–making process issued on June 14, 1927.

I have led tour groups on field trips to the Western Reserve Library and Archives in Cleveland, Ohio, where the Garrett Morgan papers are housed. Garrett A. Morgan (1877-1963), Cleveland African American businessman, invented a belt-fastener for a sewing machine, that he sold the design for $150.00. He invented a hair straightening cream and curling comb, which permitted him to open a profitable hair refining company in 1913. He received a patent for several safety devices: breathing device that was the predecessor to the gas mask in 1914; followed by his most popular electric traffic signal, which displayed green, yellow and red signs and sold to General Electric Company for $40,000 in 1923. In 1809, a native of Maryland George Peake (1722-1827) moved from Pennsylvania to Cleveland, Ohio, where he was recognized as the first African American permanent resident. There he invented a labor-saving stone hand-mill for grinding grain, which earned him the reputation as a highly respected citizen, though he did not receive a patent.

Just How Did Inventors Open Wide the Freedom Floodgate?

Scholars note the activism of African American scientists and inventors in the abolition of slavery. Benjamin Banneker (1731-1806), African American mathematician, astronomer and scientist, crafted the first clock made in America from wood and penknife that kept perfect time for forty years. He published several almanacs having himself completed and had verified all the mathematical calculations. He wrote a letter to the then Secretary of the State Thomas Jefferson in which he challenged Jefferson's views on the innate inferiority of African Americans.

The accomplishments of notable African Americans scientists, inventors and writers added credence to the claims of African American intelligence made by abolitionists. Owner of one of the larger clothing stores Thomas L. Jennings, acquired considerable wealth through his process for refurbishing clothing, which he used in the struggle to abolish slavery, to end peonage, and he also wrote protest letters. He traveled in a circle with prominent African American abolitionist Frederick Douglass (1818-1895), having written his obituary, published in the *Anglo-African Magazine*.

Wealthy Philadelphia businessman and African American abolitionist, James Forten (1766-1842) invented a sail-moving device for which he did not acquire a patent. He refused to sell his device to slave ships, organized through written letters and protests against limitations on African American settlement in Pennsylvania and opposed the American Colonization Society, an organization that promoted emigration to Africa.

Why Is It Difficult To Identify the Race of Inventors and Patentees?

I have written about the leadership role of African American inventors and patentees for African *American Leadership: A Concise Reference Guide* (Mission Bell Media, 2015). The policy of the

United States Patent Office (USPO), established in 1790, was not to report patentee's race. The unusual circumstance of the race being recorded for African American inventor of a corn seed planter Harry Blair (circa 1807-1860), by the patent examiner in 1836 led scholars, erroneously, to assume this entry represented the first African American to acquire a patent. New York City businessman and abolitionist, Thomas L. Jennings (1791-1859) received a patent for a turpentine dry cleaning process in 1821 and holds the distinction as the first African American patentee. African American inventors did not always acquire patents.

The record of African American inventors and patentees remained obscure into the twentieth century. Henry E. Baker (1857-1928), recognized as the second known African American Assistant United States Patent Officer and a law school graduate, constructed a historical record through documentation. He argued sectors of society were unaware about the contributions of African American inventors and evidence two particular events: A U.S. Congressional candidate argued that African Americans had not earned the right to vote because African Americans had not earned one patent in 1903. A major southern newspaper reported African Americans were not responsible for any inventions. He mentioned two official requests of the USPO for information about African American inventors and patentees made by African American community leaders as the reason for a research study.

I Want the Real McKoy to Got Shoes on My Feet

The term the real McCoy, meaning you wanted the genuine one, entered the American vocabulary due to his pioneering work. Elijah McCoy (1844-1929), African American mechanical engineer, became widely known for the automatic lubricating system, which made it possible to operate engines with no longer having to stop to oil, thereby saving valuable time and money. Elijah McCoy, who studied mechanical engineering in Scotland, earlier worked as a fireman for the Michigan Central Railroad where he invented a drip cup lubricating system in 1872. This lubricating device, which was modified to use in numerous other industries, helped to make this country an industrial leader. The term the real McCoy, meaning you wanted the genuine one, entered the American vocabulary due to the pioneering work of Elijah McCoy.

An immigrant from Dutch Guiana, Jan Erst Matzliger (1852-1889), received a patent for the shoe lasting machine, which provided a mechanized means to tie the sole to the upper of the shoe in 1883. Through his machine he increased the output of up to 700 shoes per day, reduced the cost of shoe production by fifty percent and made the cost of shoes more affordable.

African American inventor of a hair processing in 1905, Madam C.J. Walker became the first female African American millionaire. Yet, with all of this said my undergraduate students continue to find it amazing that a powerful nineteenth-century Black woman Maria Stewart in Boston existed and spoke of the value of science.

Excerpts from Maria Stewart's Speech in Boston on September 21, 1832.

I have heard much respecting the horrors of slavery; but may Heaven forbid that the generality of my color throughout these United States should experience any more of its horrors than to be a servant of servants, or hewers of wood and drawers of water! Tell us no more of southern slavery; for with few exceptions, although I may be very erroneous in my opinion, yet I consider our condition but little better than that. Yet, after all, methinks there are no chains so galling as the chains of ignorance—no fetters so binding as those that bind the soul, and exclude it from the vast field of useful and scientific knowledge...

Maria Stewart was the first woman of any race to give an address before men and women, Black and white in the nation. "Why of all places the turf of the New England Patriots?" got students wondering.

Notes

Barksdale-Hall, Roland C. *African American Inventive Genius: James Elmer Matthews (1886-1976) and William Hunter Dammond (1873-1956)*. Mercer, Pennsylvania: Mercer County Historical Society, 1995.

Finkebine, Roy E. *Sources of the African American Past: Primary Sources in American History*. New York: Pearson Education, 2004, pp.31-33.

Kings-Meadow, Tyson D., ed. *African American Leadership: A Reference Guide*. Santa Barbara, CA: Mission Bell Media, 2015.

Wright, Michelle Diane. *Broken Utterances: A Selected Anthology of 19th Century Black Women's Social Thought*. Baltimore, MD; Three Sistas Press, 2007.

Life Applications

1. What challenges might you face in achieving your goal?

2. What strategies might you employ to reach your goal?

3. Write your dream down. Don't be apprehensive about writing down your dream. It is o.k. if you have gotten off the track in the past. It now is time to get back on track. Post the dream on the wall or somewhere visible were you can it see daily.

Chapter Four
Black Bostonians' Literary Gifts and Power

Does a Kernel of Truth Multiply?

It is a myth that all enslaved persons were manumitted by the kindness of masters. A string of Massachusetts legal decisions that lasted more than two decades resulted in the Quok Walker case, which ended Massachusetts slavery in 1783. In Massachusetts free Blacks and enslaved Africans agitated for better living conditions and participated in protests. In 1773, several Massachusetts enslaved persons circulated a protest document that sought increased freedom. Lawsuits were more common than normally known in the upper South and North. New England slavery, which Puritans modeled after mosaic traditions, permitted some legal rights and operated quite different from the lower South.

My undergraduate students have noted similarities between what Maria W Stewart, a Black feminist, depicted in Boston some more than 170 years ago and the current situation in the ghetto.

Excerpts from Maria Stewart's Speech in Boston on September 21, 1832.

> *…. Do you ask, why are you wretched and miserable? I reply, look at many of the most worthy and interesting of us doomed to spend our lives in gentlemen's kitchens. Look at our young men, smart, active and energetic, with souls filled with ambitious fire; if they look forward, alas!what are their prospects? They can be nothing but the humblest laborers, on account of their dark complexions; hence many of them lose their ambition, and become worthless. Look at our middle-aged men, clad in their rusty plaids and coats; in*

winter, every cent they earn goes to buy their wood and pay their rents; their poor wives also toil beyond their strength, to help support their families. Look at our aged sires, whose heads are whitened with the front of seventy winters, with their old wood-saws on their backs. Alas, what keeps us so? Prejudice, ignorance and poverty....

Quok Walker, Maria Stewart, Phillis Wheatley, Crispus Attucks, and Prince Hall dropped kernels of truth in their time.

We owe a debt of gratitude to the literary gifts of Phillis Wheatley, an enslaved African, who in her own meek way challenged racism. She showed a mastery of English, though it was her second language. She was questioned when she wrote her book of poems. White folks challenged Black intelligence and still do today. Said Black folks could not be free because they were not intelligent enough to handle freedom. Just could not believe the gal had brains. Well, Phillis was interrogated about her language arts skills by a panel of white males. Under fire Phillis passed the test and her book of poetry was published. She opened the freedom door for us all. You go girl!

Elnora Fortson (front row, far), founder of Praise Poets, the author (back row, far right), wife Drusilla (2nd row, middle) with performance group at Hill House in Pittsburgh;

Crispus Attucks Early Learning Center, located at 50 East Boundary Avenue in York, Pennsylvania, represents advancement in services.

We are beneficiaries of a poetic legacy, beginning with Phillis Wheatley. My wife and I, along with a college friend Donna Walker, belonged to a lively poetry group. The Praise Poets, founded by Eleanor Fortson, meeting at a Black church in Pittsburgh's Friendship neighborhood provided our entry into performance poetry. Sister Phyllis would recite Paul Laurence Dunbar. We belonged to the Federal Poets in Washington, DC.

Phillis Wheatley fought for freedom in a more reserved manner than Crispus Attucks. Today the name of Crispus Attucks is honored in American history. There are schools, apartment buildings, community centers and playgrounds named in his honor. Crispus Attucks, the first casualty of the Boston Massacre, became the first martyr in the American Revolution. Some years prior the October 2, 1750 *Boston Gazette* carried an ad for him as a runaway: "Ran away from his master *William Brown of Framingham* on the 30th of *Sept.* last, a Molatto fellow, about 27 Years of Age, named Crispas, 6 Feet two Inches, short curl'd Hair, his Knees nearer together than common: had on a light coulor'd Bearskin Coat..." William Brown listed a ten-pound reward, but Crispus alluded capture. In 1858, Black abolitionists in Boston commemorated a Crispus Attucks Day in his honor.

One of the early memories I have is speaking for Black History Month at the Crispus Attucks Center in York, Pennsylvania. Founded in 1931, the Crispus Attucks Community Center currently is located at 605 S. Duke Street, has a proud history as a social change agent in the community. In 1969, York experienced racial unrest. Two people died in the riots. A history of the Crispus Attucks Center currently is being written. In recent times I revisited the Crispus Attucks Center. One of the newest additions to York City's landscape is the Crispus Attucks Early Learning Center, serving more than 200 youth in York County, located at 50 Boundary Street across from the Crispus Attucks Community Center.

Meeting Needs through Black Self-Help in Boston

Black Bostonians James Oliver Horton and Lois E. Horton portrayed an eighteenth-century Black population which faced many challenges. During the eighteenth and nineteenth century few of Boston's Blacks owned land. Yet the problem went even deeper than lack of private ownership of land, for even those Blacks who just wanted to rent a room found themselves very much restricted. There was a housing shortage among Boston's Black community. The Blacks were also faced with high unemployment. In the winter months they were faced with limited shelter, high clothing expenditures, and the added costs of firewood. Boston's Black community developed extensive survival networks in order to cope with the needs and problems of Boston's Blacks.

Boston's Black community responded to the need for more housing. Black families began to take in boarders. Taking in boarders probably stemmed from both custom, and economic and social necessity. The extra income brought in by the rent which the boarder paid, gave the Black families sagging economy a boost. So in fact the boarder was at times helping the family as much as the family was helping the boarder. Taking in boarders also was a manifestation on the responsibility many blacks felt for one another, for the Black community had always tried to provide services to fellow

Blacks who were unable to get these services elsewhere. Besides renting rooms in Black households, black boarders found lodging in the few black-operated boardinghouses. This black communal strategy effectively dealt with the housing shortage encountered by Blacks.

The Black family within the limits of its household arrangement did very much to help the Blacks of Boston to cope with their problems. Besides taking in boarders, the Black family took in homeless children. This was a civic duty not limited to the financially stable. This practice was also important among Boston's Blacks, since Boston's institutions for homeless children did not admit Black children. The Black family taking in the homeless Black children adequately met the Black child's needs The Black family's strategies to cope with different community needs appeared to have been very successful.

Black women dealt with key issues. Women met and formed patrols to do something about loud noises made by children going to and from school. They also formed loosely structured groups which addressed such issues as temperance, unemployment, and needed community services. They did get some things accomplished; however, they were not as successful as the Black family working together. These groups formed by Black women were also limited because they had limited organizational structure.

There were several organized Black institutions. Where possible, Blacks established institutions to serve their needs, supplementing the family's role and binding the Black people into a community. Blacks used the Church as an agent of protest. The church was also a training ground for leaders, a place for the education and training of the young, a place of entertainment and social life, and a meeting place for exchange of thoughts. Church involvement afforded social stability. The church was successful in helping the black community of Boston to cope with a hostile social environment.

Why Networks Make a Difference?

Now Pops belonged to Twin City Elks Independent Benevolent and Protective Order of Elks of the World (IBPOEW) Lodge in Farrell but he loved Masonry. Mr. Jefferson likely sponsored Pops to join Calumet Lodge 25 Free and Accepted Masons, Prince Hall Affiliation in Farrell, Pennsylvania. My paper, "The Twin City Elks Lodge, A Unifying Force in Farrell's African American Community," won the 1993 Pennsylvania Museum and Historical Museum Black History Conference Essay Contest. Graduate research at Duquesne University focused upon a twentieth century development, the Twin City Elks Lodge in Mercer County, though it left a lasting impression of the proactive role played by African Americans, if sometimes overlooked, in community building.

Twin City, the largest Black Elks lodge in the state of Pennsylvania with membership over seven hundred for almost twenty years between 1940 and 1960, built a $75,000 gymnasium and saw a great advancement equated with "racial pride." The Twin City Lodge also sponsored beneficial activities for young people, which included basketball, roller skating, a drum and bugle corps, majorettes, a marching band, and a youth council. During the Christmas season the Black Elks provided treats for children and spent two to three hundred dollars on charitable works in the Black community. They also sponsored a softball team for adults; arranged field trips to Pittsburgh and Cleveland; and held raffles, picnics and cabarets. The lodge's club held floor shows and attracted such celebrities as Duke Ellington, Ray Charles, Peg Leg Bates and Jesse Owens. The availability of steady work and decent wages enabled the community to support these Elks-sponsored activities. A national dignitary, the dynamic J. Finley Wilson, traveled across the country "telling people, 'If you want to see somebody with money, go to Farrell, Pennsylvania.'" For more on this topic and photos, see Chapter Five "Farrell's Twin City Elks Lodge, A Unifying Force" in my book *African Americans in Mercer County* (Arcadia Publishing, 2009).

The Black Masons were no slouches either. Pops rose to become fraternal leader in the Masons. At his invitation I later joined the Odell B. Matthews Sr. Council 11 Order of Knights of Pythagoras, Free and Accepted Masons, Prince Hall Affiliation in Farrell, Pennsylvania. Those Black Masons in the names of Odell B. Matthews, Jr, Alexander Cromartie, David Myers and Ralph Jefferson were not just youth boosters but became lifelong mentors and friends. The female auxiliary Mother Advisor Martha Cromartie, an African American public school teacher, provided guidance. When I became an adult I had a standing appointment for storytelling with the youth department.

Prince Hall was a founding father of African American fraternal life. He opened the door for Black fraternal life in many ways. He came in through a British lodge because white folks in in the United States did not want to initiate a Black person. In Boston the African Masonic Lodge met some of the community's physical needs. The lodge handed out free firewood during the winter and sponsored periodic food drives for those in need. Weekly "sick dues" were provided for members unable to work and loans were made to members and their families. Prince Hall's pioneering spirit opened doors for folks to join Masonic lodges, other lodges, fraternities and sororities.

Other Black institutions filled a social and economic void felt by blacks. Another institution, the African Society, a mutual aid and charity organization, provided social welfare to its members and their families. Support was also provided to widows, orphans, and infirms by the African Society. Other organizations such as the Adelphic Union Library Association encouraged intellectual debates and offered lectures. Boston's Blacks practiced self-help attempted to cope with their problems. We inherit a love of freedom, protest, social network and racial uplift tradition, beginning in Boston.

PITTSBURGH

May 19, 1993
Vol 23 No. 172

Renaissance News

the community newspaper

Reaching 120,000 African-Americans in Allegheny County every week

Local Historian Wins State Competition

Roland C. Barksdale-Hall

As a Duquesne University graduate student, Roland C. Barksdale-Hall wrote his winning essay, "The Twin City Elks Lodge of Farrell: An African American Community Agent, 1909-1944."

The Pennsylvania Historical and Museum Commission chose this essay as the winning graduate entry in the 1993 Black History Conference Essay Contest. As a winner, Barksdale receives a $200 prize and the opportunity for publication, and he presented his essay to this year's Conference on Black History in Pennsylvania held last week in Williamsport, PA.

Now, history is a career for Roland C. Barksdale-Hall,

executive director of the Western Pennsylvania African American Historical and Genealogical Society. A member of Phi Alpha Theta, the international honorary society in history, Barksdale has master's degrees in American History from Duquesne University and library science from the University of Pittsburgh.

Barksdale, listed in Who's Who among Black Americans, serves as the national vice president for History on the board of directors of the Afro-American Historical and Genealogical Society and on the board of directors of the Allegheny City Society. He currently represents The Carnegie Library of Pittsburgh on the board of directors of I Dream a World, an interdisciplinary approach to multi-cultural education.

Barksdale's poetry on historical themes has appeared in several publications. He has had several articles published and has pursued graduate studies in publishing at George Washington University, Washington, DC, and is a frequent speaker on historical and genealogical topics.

Pittsburgh Renaissance News announces author as a winner of state history competition;

Author (back row, third from left) was a youth presenter in Flower Talk program sponsored by Prince Hall Masonic Lodge, where youth group honored grandmothers, mothers and sisters in our community.

Why Do Thugs Emerge?

Non-traditional students have contrasted and compared the stupor-state men who walked around in search of wood in nineteenth-century Boston and the look in today's urban communities. In the twenty-first century Tony Rose fleshes out how thugs emerge from a state of survival in Black America, where basic food, safety and human nurturance falls in short supply. The uncensored autobiography of legendary gold and platinum record music producer and book publishing mogul, Tony Rose, NAACP Image Award winner, tells you how in an R-rated, due to violence, sexual abuse, language, rape, drugs and rage style. In a riveting, makes you wanna holler…searing indictment of America in the "benign neglect" of a dog-eat-dog world, where the alpha dog preys on the weak in Roxbury/Boston's Whittier Street Housing Projects, where Black males going to the lockup becomes a passé rite-of-passage to manhood.

His careening life-and-death course between the criminal underworld and a caring world for America's underclass, represented by a hustler father, scoutmaster, nuns and priest, military, business leader and a transformation, that leaves you holding on to your pants. America is indebted to Mr. Rose for writing this biting, brutally-honest, wake-up call masterpiece. For more on this topic of urban survival, read Tony's Rose's biting biography *America The Black Point of View: An Investigation and Study of the White People of America and Western Europe and The Autobiography of an American Ghetto Boy The 1950's and 1960's.* Tony Rose gives us concrete steps to become part of the solution through his newly found foundation for disadvantaged youth in the projects, ghettos and rural reaches before a new generation of thugs emerge. Hopefully, Tony Rose's valiant efforts to champion better opportunities for disadvantaged youth and save our children's lives can multiply.

Notes

Finkebine, Roy E. *Sources of the African American Past: Primary Sources in American History.* New York: Pearson Education, 2004, pp.31-33.

Horton, James Oliver and Horton, Lois E. *Black Bostonians.* New York, Holmes and Meier, 1979.

Rose, Tony. *America The Black Point of View An Investigation and Study of the White People of America and Western Europe and the Autobiography of a Ghetto Boy the 1950's and 1960's.* Phoenix, AZ: Amber Books, 2015.

Wright, Michelle Diane. *Broken Utterances: A Selected Anthology of 19th Century Black Women's Social Thought.* Baltimore, MD; Three Sistas Press, 2007.

Life Applications

1. Who offers a sense of belonging in today's community?

2. What kernel of truth do you value and would you like to pass on and see multiply?

3. What organizations do you and family members share a common bond? What does the bond mean to you?

4. Who are underserved populations in your community? How do the Black church and mosques reach underserved populations in your community?

5. What might we do to improve on the feeling of sense of belonging in our communities?

PART II
Communicating in Tough Times

Chapter Five
Navigating Emotional Minefields

Will You Stay the Course?

Rent Parties
(A TRIBUTE TO LANGSTON HUGHES)

Honey, she's gone…
Blowing her horn like Joshua
around the walls…
As much noise
as she's made
And as many parties
as she's thrown
If we do the polka every night she
can't
say anything
…I know where
I might have made her mad
when I said
"Kiss my ass"

And she said
"Who's that talking to me?"
…And I haven't seen her since

At another time we stood formidable. Right after Momma passed, we enlisted in the Army Reserves. Poppa had passed three years earlier. Off to Fort Dix we went for basic training. After the induction we lost our hair, dropped the civvies and received a round of shots. Packed in a cattle car we poured out to hit the ground. Give me thirty pushups. Welcome to the Army.

Inside the barracks we scurried to find a bunk. Rooms with less bunks at the one end of the hall existed. We realized. So we hauled our butt in that direction. We ran through the door. Great, it had two bunks. Right behind us ran in Mike, a skinny white fellow. We detected a southern accent. Where in the South? We were not sure.

"How is this going to work?" We wondered. Well, we had made up our minds we were not going anywhere. And Mike looked like he was there to stay as well.

Mike was stressed about his buzzed haircut more than we did. He had a hard time doing 30 pushups. One time he did not make the pushups and turned all red in the face. We kept him going telling him 'yes you can do the pushups'.

We struggled together. Together we such had long classes that we almost could fall asleep. Except we were invited to stand up the first time we dozed. We went through the gas that burned our eyes and made us unable to breathe. We ate tuna from cans with sand in it from what a passerby kicked in it out on the range. We got so cold and wet where we could not feel our hands and feet. We bivouacked, putting up a tent, digging a foxhole and searching to find sand to cover it.

Author in basic training at Fort Dix

We developed camaraderie. On the ten-mile hike Mike lost his weapon and the drill sergeant found it. He was deep in trouble. On the confidence course Mike and I were the last to come down from the scaffold. Mike was on the second floor when I got my leg pinned on the highest floor and was hanging upside down. Mike fought to climb back up there and save my life. There was an inspection and Mike did not have a bag tied to his bunk. We found our bunk and bedding out in the hall. We had to clean the latrine floor with a toothbrush. By then we had become buddies. We were able to laugh about our dilemma, but not in front of the drill sergeant.

Who Said That?

"Bastard!" Somebody called out from formation.

"Who said that?" The drill sergeant yelled. Nobody stepped forward.

So we all suffered. We ran from one end of the barracks and did pushups to the other end and did pushups for a long time.

Well, Mike and I stood tall, even when the hot sun was beaming down on us, in our Class A's uniform. Unlike the hostile soldier, who cursed at the drill sergeant and preferred jail time rather than disciplined living. We became friends. You see, we prevailed together, completed the course and still remain friends.

Author and Army buddy Mike in Class A's

Are We More At Risk In the Hood Than the Military?

OMG, Bam! Bam! Bam! 9 mm bullets ripped through the blinds. We were right in the line of fire. Were this a battlefield simulation I might have taken cover, found a better tactical position, repealed the enemy. "Get on the Ground!" I barked to my friend, Jackie. I knew everybody by name. Thank God, all the women left. I was doing what became a passion "Tracing Your Roots Seminar" at the public housing library.

"Are we more at risk in the hood than the military?" I wondered. It was thirty-five years later. I weighed fifteen pounds more. So I was not quite ready to roll. It was 1:45 p.m. I called 911. What the heck! Jackie was not moving! He sat right at the same table in the confusion, just talking like nothing was happening.

The dust began to settle. "Fortunately, this was a school day." I thought. "How can America ignore the violence?" The stray bullets had gone right through the area where our children played Kinect. I still was in a daze. The shock was just setting in.

"Do I have the courage to come back?"

Quinby Street Resource Center

As earlier mentioned, three years ago, when I became the library director at the public housing we did not know the rewarding yet challenging experience it would be. Stuff goes down in the ghetto. I knew the children and adults needed the services we offered at the center.

It was not until days after when I looked at the bullet holes and shredded blinds in the community room did the full reality set in. The bullet holes went through the adjacent walls of the room and lodged in the other side of the hall.

I lived within walking distance of the projects. I walked to work. Yet I was far removed. We now were starting to know what the real deal was. I had to seek inner guidance to look into the real world. I gained valuable lessons that became building blocks of emotional literacy. According to Robert K. Cooper in *Executive EQ: Emotional Intelligence in Leadership and Organizations*, emotional literacy helps us to "be real and true to [ourselves]: builds personal power—including self-awareness, inner guidance, respect, responsibility, and connection" (1).

Some are walking the tight rope. Others are dangling by a thread. I have had folks just come in and just break down. Young mothers, who are working hard to raise their children, are stressed. Those are so tired. I hear some cursing at their kids.

Youth are shooting at each other in the real world. One was shot and killed at a birthday party celebration. Somebody just was *shot in the thigh,* in the thigh after an argument as the book goes to press. No peace on earth, even during the Holiday Season. "Are you tired yet?" was on a flyer circulated to residents for a special called meeting. You wonder why some get a buzz now and then to escape stress.

Why Consider an Alternate Route?

Yet alternate routes to freedom exist in the ghetto, though alternate routes to freedom are not easy. In recent times, a strategy frequently used to discredit good ideas and Imhotep Institution Builders has been to attack the person's reputation. I have witnessed mentoring programs for our youth come under fire due to attacks on a person's race or background. In critical thinking we call this ad hominem, a Latin term, which means to attack the person. We have seen attacks on a person's reputation skillfully employed by Congress persons to scuttlebutt legislation.

Folks, we got to put on our thinking caps. It is of utmost importance that we stop letting folk discredit positive programming and progressive leadership in our community. Students in our Africana literature classes have found an exercise to be beneficial. We compare and contrast the various press coverage about Malcolm X's assassination. We find the lesson an eye opener about point of view in reporting.

Why We Cannot Afford the "Isms" To Run Over Us?

Progressive thinkers face challenges on many fronts. Today, I would not change my life for the whole world. I now live in the real world. I have found hostility to progressive ideas in the halls of academia. I have written about the hostility I experienced at Pennsylvania State University in my chapter, "Building Dialogic Bridges to Diversity: Are We There Yet?" in *Where Are All the Librarians of Color?: The Experiences of People of Color in Academia* (Library Juice Press 2015).

"Must have been kids" going down the street policeman told us. I said, "Ride down the street. There is not another house with paint blasted over it and painted hand prints." Yet we did not argue. We got to pick our battles.

Now, we were discouraged when our home was blasted by paint bullets at night. Painted hand-prints were left on the front porch. Our children thought it was real bullets and were afraid. We have endured other folks' barbs, taunts and lack of enlightenment from some quarters, as might be expected. A few grassroots supporters came by and encouraged us.

"Well, that's what happens to activists." Our African American neighbor quickly responded and shrugged his shoulders. Our local newspaper refused to cover what had happened. So I shelled money out of our pocket for an ad which ran in the local newspaper *The (Sharon, Pennsylvania) Herald.*

> **FIFTY DOLLAR REWARD**
> On Friday, May 18, 2001, around 11:00 pm., my Sharon family home was paint-blasted while my family was home. More than 40 paint-bullets were shot at my white house. Painted hand-prints were left on the front porch. Orange and green bullets hit three of my front windows and damaged the front and side of our white siding. After cleaning, the paint continues to bleed from under the siding.
> A police report was made. I am offering a fifty dollar re-ward to anyone who has any information, leading to the arrest and conviction of responsible parties.
> Roland Barksdale-Hall
> 939 Baldwin Ave., Sharon.

Newspaper ad offering reward for info about attack on home.

I am a witness to the fact that a cost remains for community activism. Still, the truth be told, righteousness will prevail in the long run. So it is not time to pack up our bags and go home. I cannot afford to allow the "isms"—racism, eurocentrism, sexual orientation, sexism and classism—in any form hold us back. I am ever indebted to our community for insights gained, in particular the lessons on resilience.

Notes

Cooper, R. K. *Executive EQ: Emotional Intelligence in Leadership and Organizations.* New York, Perigree Book, 1986.

Goleman, Daniel. *Working with Emotional Intelligence.* New York: Bantam Books, 1998.

Life Applications

1. How have your family members coped with hardship? Were the strategies effective or ineffective? Why or why not? What calms you in the time of trouble? What challenges have you faced on your journey? How do you deal with hurt and disappointment?

2. What milestones or markers have you had in your life? Make a timeline of your life. Record important events. Why do you view these moments as significant?

Chapter Six
Life After Trayvon

Q&A with Sharon Flake

Sharon Flake, teen author of the Skin I' m In, and I have presented together at Pitt Homecoming events and the Pittsburgh Children's Book Festival in the Hill District. In conversations about the real word we have found Sharon Flake to be a kindred spirit. I had done a popular interview with Sharon Flake, "Life After Trayvon," that topped the May-June 2012 QBR Black Book Review list of headline stories. The Q&A session with Sharon Flake remains on the hot topics list:

Author with children's authors Sharon Flake, Elizabeth Howard, and Kelly Starling Lyon at Ujamma Collective Children's Literary Festival in Pittsburgh's Hill District.

Q: What has been the response to *The Skin I'm In?*

SF: *The Skin I'm In* is my oldest, bestselling novel. There are over a million in print. It has been published in French (called Black Blues), and is used in colleges, elementary, middle and high schools around the country. Regularly I get e-mails from children and parents saying how the novel helped with their self-esteem. One girl's mom recently said that her daughter created a board game from it.

In Minneapolis there is an organization called Lovin' the Skin I'm In Youth Development Initiative http://www.invergrove.k12.mn.us/lovin.html which helps girls build their self-esteem and strengthen their character in a number of ways… it's not my organization, but the book and an innovative sister named Robin Hickman http://hrusa.org/closethegap/educator/race/skin.php helped get it off the ground.

Q: How do you stay so well in sync with the voice of today's youth culture?

SF: I am not sure myself. I think we know, however, many of the issues are impacting youth simply by watching television or reading any newspaper. There is also my gut, intuition, and belief that there is more to youth than we give them credit for.

Q: Who inspired you to write?

SF: I tell people that I am a writer in spite of myself. I started in college after discovering I wasn't very good at much else. But I couldn't spell and didn't know the rules of grammar—well, so I thought I wasn't a good writer—even though professors were giving me good grades.

I had an opportunity to do an internship at a major, local newspaper and never showed up. They called me three times. I promised to come, but I knew I wouldn't.

I was sure I was a bad writer and they were just being nice to me. After I graduated, I don't know why, but I felt like God wanted me to be a writer.

"He could do better than to pick someone who couldn't spell," I was thinking. I remember crying and wishing the feeling that I was supposed to be a writer would just go away.

I gave in though, mostly to shut God up! I'm glad that nagging feeling that I was called to walk this way didn't go anyplace. And I'm glad for friends who were committed writers, because watching them and being around them helped me find my way to where I am today.

Now, I get to talk to thousands of kids who feel like they aren't good enough, who are afraid to dream. Or who don't even see their worth and talent. And I get to say:

"I know who you are. You are just like me. And you can fly, even higher than I, if you believe, and just keep on walking in your gift."

Q: Why did you write *You Don't Even Know Me: Stories and Poems About Boys?*

SF: I wrote it for two reasons, one very practical. I was struggling with a longer novel and felt that a shorter format would help me to get unstuck. I have always written about young African American males, mainly because I think their stories still go largely untold. Or if there is a story to be told by them, it primarily is told through the lens of a camera and reported on the six o'clock news.

I wanted to explore young males from a variety of perspectives. To have them in my novels have conversations that don't always take place as they should. To have them read my work and see themselves and talk about themselves in any ways they would like. A young boy gets married in my novel. Another boy attempts suicide.

In a note to me last year, a professor told me that her student teacher taught from this book. As a result of reading it, one of the teenage male students in class wrote a letter saying he was being abused. The book tackles some heavy, interesting, topics.

But it is also as much about fathers as it is about young men. Surrogate fathers, adoptive fathers, grandfathers and more. They give sage, wise advice, and not so good advice. I am always excited to hear what boys think about the book. They usually are surprised that a 56-year-old woman wrote it.

Q: What special memories do you hold from times spent as a youth counselor?

SF: Wow, I was so young. No children. Going to folks' homes and working with them on how best to help young people navigate school, foster care and often difficult home lives. Mostly I remember how important it was for me to do a good job, and to help young people get back home to their families, which was the primary goal. And to support the young people in any way I could, and to make sure they were safe where they were and protected.

I have a pretty good gut, so mostly I went by that when I worked with families. It's also the way I write. I never know where I am going, how the story will turn. I only have a gem of an idea. I want to write about boys. And then I get on the bike and ride.

Q: Is there a message to the front cover of *You Don't Even Know Me*, showing a boy with a hoodie on and holding a physics notebook?

SF: Yeah. The original picture had a boy with a spray can in his hand. I saw it and said, "No that won't do." It reinforces what people think they know about kids like him. I wanted the physics book because I knew that people think they know guys in hoodies already. I wanted to confirm what my lead poem said— "You don't know me no matter how many newspapers you read. You don't know what I am fully capable of, what I dream about."

I am from Philly. A few years ago I went to an elementary school there to discuss my book, *The Broken Bike Boy and the Queen of 33rd Street.* I asked the students if anyone knew a king or queen in their neighborhood. A young 5th grader said he was a king.

"What do you do that would tell us you are a king?" I asked him. He said he made breakfast for his mother on weekends. I asked what sort of king that made him.

"A loyal king," he said. The teacher, principal and librarian beamed, and were stunned. They never knew this about him. "You Don't Even Know Me" he was saying, without even knowing it.

It's why I love what I do. Young folks say things during my talks and questions that their teachers and peers do not know about them. One kid had a grandfather in Africa, who was a king. Again his class never knew.

Q: What has been the impact of the Trayvon Martin case?

SF: We do not yet know what the full impact will be. What we do know is that people of all ethnic backgrounds, professions and genders decided that the killing of Trayvon Martin was so egregious that they had to speak up, march, sign petitions and make their voices heard. Now the hard work begins. Not simply in the courtroom for Trayvon's lawyers and family, but in our communities, schools and homes.

For America will be on trial as well. Many, many of us read the op-eds, and listened to the discussions and debates about what Black boys face in America. Now what will we do with this knowledge? How can we remain the same?

How many Trayvon's must die before we as a nation truly believe that all of our children are valuable?

The impact of the Trayvon Martin shooting can be life altering for boys of color in this country, if we have the courage to take on some really important issues: guns and violence, illiteracy, self-esteem, cultural and family dynamics, school dropout rates and the big one—the impact of slavery on present day generations. It will take all hands on deck to deal with these issues and help young Black males be all that they were created to be. But if we accept the challenge, the entire nation benefits—even young people who look nothing like Trayvon.

Q: Do you sense a difference in life before Trayvon?

SF: Americans have been silent for decades, watching African American youth die through the hands of police, Black males, and others. I wrote the novel *Bang!* several years ago because of my concern that the Trayvon Martins of the world—African American youth—were being shot and killed with most of the country seemingly okay with it. The book talks about the impact of violence on youth and families.

When I go to schools and ask young people how many of them know someone who has been shot and killed, it is typical for 80-90 percent of the hands to go up. One teacher told me of an angry sixth grader in her class. After a while, she had a conversation with him. It turned out his father, step-father and I believe his brother, had all been shot and killed at some point in his life. I suspect it might be hard to pay attention in school, to learn and want more for yourself when you are forever grieving or think the next gun might be aimed at you.

Q: What, if any, ray of hope exists?

SF: Hope has always been present, even during the Holocaust and slavery there were those who remained hopeful. I am hopeful that now that our eyes have been opened, we will work together for the betterment of Black youth.

That happens not just through marching, but volunteering, working to change policies on a local, state and national level, and improving schools. It also happens by getting books into the hands of young people. I cannot tell you how the right book can heal, offer hope to a young person who believes they have none, or make him feel significant when so much around him says he isn't.

Q: What is your goal?

SF: My goal always is to break young people out of boxes. To have folks see them as fully as possible, but not as perfect beings, for none of us is. It is the tension between my characters' strengths and weaknesses that draw people to them.

I have about two million books in print. I get letters from young people in China, Vietnam, South America, Africa, the Caribbean, Ireland, Australia and elsewhere. I am having the time of my life.

Q: What message would you like to leave?

SF: I want your readers to know that everybody matters. Everyone has a gift. No one is perfect…and that hard work and a helping hand towards others will help you create a wonderful life for yourself and those you love. Sharon Flake website: http://www.sharongflake.com/

Life Applications

1. Do you know anybody who was shot?

2. How might we change future outcomes in our community?

PART III
Teaching Ancestors and the Counter-Narrative History

Chapter Seven
Researching Our Roots

Why Is It Liberational?

homecoming
warm embrace
love basked
sincerity clothed
soul food

In Steeler Country we received the Afro-American Historical and Genealogical Society James Dent Walker Award, the highest award bestowed for accomplishments in support of the AAHGS mission and significant contributions to the research, documentation and preservation of African American history. It was even more meaningful to receive it at the Three Rivers, because this was my home where we founded the AAHGS Pittsburgh Chapter.

Special people from life surrounded me. On the same evening my mentor Sylvia Cooke Martin a visionary leader and pioneer during the formative stages of AAHGS chapter development received the AAHGS Distinguished Service Award. My mentee Vernon Scott was the recipient of the Debra Newman Ham Education Award. I took a photograph with the other awardees.

(l-r) Author, Sylvia Cooke Martin and Vernon Scott received awards at the AAHGS National Conference held in Pittsburgh.

Where Do You Come From?

I was invited for a segment on Family Reunions. Madonna Chism Pinkard, host of WFMJ-TV Community Connection, had interrupted the show to tell my son's story. She read "Your son received 1st place at Sharon High School in a trigonometry contest with a score of 94 out of 100 and a time of 43 minutes. He scored third highest in Pennsylvania." Madonna thought this was extraordinary and in keeping with my rich family tradition of excellence.

Emmanual African Methodist Episcopal Church

The Cousin Coming Together :

A Memoir of the Barksdale - Massey Family

And in you shall all the Families of earth shall be blessed

Genesis 12 : 3

Reverend   Arthur Brown ,   Pastor

Home   334 - 687- 2487

Reverend David E. Redd ick , Presiding Elder
Bishop James L. Davis ,   Presiding Prelate

Family reunion program at St. Emmanuel A.M.E. Church in Eufaula, Alabama

Madonna returned to the topic of the show and asked me about family reunion planning. I shared about a successful community-based cultural program in Eufaula, Alabama I had done. The *Eufaula Eagle* was intrigued by my background and local connections. The Alabama newspaper carried a story, "African Cultural Program Tapped for Library." "The Cousins Coming Together" program included storytelling, seminars on tracing your roots and tips on staying healthy and planning reunions. The community program was to coincide with my Barksdale Massey family reunion.

Do Misconceptions about Being "Poor" Exist?

I showed Madonna, the hostess of Community Connections, a vintage photograph of my Big Momma Camilla, Great Aunt Clemmy and Cousin Karen in front of the corral. "Roland, I don't know how to say this. But look your story is even more amazing! Look where you came from. I mean look at their clothes. Your family was poor."

I beg to differ my people in the South were not "poor." The 1890s of Jim Crow, disfranchisement through poll taxes and grandfather clauses, lynching, and the rise of the KKK ushered in what historians termed a low point in African American history. DuBois' classic *The Souls of Black Folk* (1903) finally forecasted the problem of the Twentieth Century to be the "color-line." Beyond adversity, my people framed a belief and value system.

My family was not alone. The name Camilla comes from Latin and means free-born and noble. Those folks lived by 'a house was not a home'. It was what you filled it with.

I have had to hip my students as well. In the classroom I shared a photo taken in front of Great Aunt Clemmy's home on the dirt road. One gave a shout-out. "That's one of those sharecropper places!" This caught all of their attention. It was like they had opened a time capsule. The wonder in their eyes told it all. It was plain to see. Students pondered "How Professor Barksdale could be one generation removed from sharecropping? How did a family fit in this simple wooden structure? How did Black folks survive?"

I shared my Momma and Pops might never have met in the Big Apple if it were not for a rattlesnake. Pops attended segregated school until about fourth grade and to his credit understood about Black survival. I hear tell back in the day he was a tough hombre, a match to a rattlesnake. Maybe this trait is what caused country folk to give him the nickname, "Black Sugar." When a rattlesnake, near the length of a sofa, bit the hell out of his leg the buck killed the snake. He made a tourniquet, got on an old bicycle and peddled.

Just to think I might not exist if it were not for that snake. "I be damn! I be damn! You done saved yourself. The White doctor exclaimed. "You either going to be a doctor or going to the military." He referred to how the poison came out through the peddling. My Pops soon was packing for the military to leave his Alabama home.

ABOVE: Mr. Barksdale-Hall on Community Connection with hostess Madonna Pinkard Chism; BELOW: Mr. Barksdale-Hall stands in front of Great Aunt Clemmy's home on the dirt road.

Big Momma Camilla, Great Aunt Clemmy and Cousin Karen in front of the corral.

"5" Core Values of Freed Persons in the South

- An education takes folks somewhere;

- Stewardship of the land;

- Sharing, as expressed through a devotion to family and neighbors;

- Commitment to the development of a viable Church, sacred and secular institutions;

- Hallmark of industry, a commitment to work hard and save.

I am a product of southern heritage. Southern migrants were rich in character and rich in good works. My humble roots go deep in the South. Yes, my family story, it would be considered the American dream. But make no mistake our story is not unique. Mr. Toby Jackson is another example of a southern migrant. Our families both hail from Eufaula, Alabama. He preceded me as a recipient of the Mercer County Unit N.A.A.C.P. James Mendez Matthews Community Service Award. I was humbled to follow in the footsteps of an African American civil rights leaders and wrote a commemorative memorial tribute about this leader published in the newspaper.

◇◇◇

Toby Jackson, A True Hero

I had the good pleasure of knowing Mr. Toby Jackson. He, like my Dad, was born in Eufaula, Alabama. In his later years Mr. Jackson loved to hear about Eufaula so when I would visit I would bring him news and share pictures. The Eufaula of their day and times was a challenging place for a Black man to mature and develop. Yet the men held no bitterness of the past and strove to help others elevate themselves in life. Race never was used as an excuse.

It was out of a deep abiding Christian faith commitment he served the community and established an impeccable record of service in the Shenango Valley. Mr. Jackson was a pillar at Morris Chapel A.M.E. Church, Farrell, where my grandparents and extended family attended. He was a Sunday School teacher and trustee. On many occasions he would be the sole African American representative on a board or committee. He served on the Farrell Planning Commission, the advisory board of McDowell Bank, and on the Pennsylvania Board of Managers. His appointment to the Farrell Area School Board in 1975 opened the door for greater minority participation. He subsequently was elected and served for nine years. He was involved in the Wiseman Organization and helped to bring the YMCA to the Shenango Valley.

Mr. Jackson was active in the Mercer County Branch N.A.A.C.P. and the recipient of its James M. Matthews Community Service Award. When I was disabled and returned back home, Mr. Jackson came to our home and repaired the porch and trap door and installed the hot water. He would only allow me to reimburse him for the materials and refused to accept a cent for his labor. He did the work of the Lord quietly and without fanfare and would be ashamed to know that I am telling this story. He was a talented tradesman, active in Habitat for Humanity, and helped many in the neighborhood.

In recent times, when I needed help with my research on my book, *African Americans in Mercer County,* Toby and his wife Dorothy Jackson shared life stories, called friends, and poured through countless photos for me at their home. Toby Jackson is an example of a generation of man that was evident around me in my youth. I am thankful to have known him. He used what God gave him to serve others throughout his life.

◇◇◇

150 Years Later: Teaching About Ancestors and Counter-Narrative History

Well, we've come a long way baby. In recent times I spoke at the Black Cultural Centers Conference, held at Auburn University. Almost seventy-five years later I returned back to Eufaula, Alabama and presented a paper, "150 Years Later: Teaching About Ancestors and Counter-Narrative History in the Social Justice Classroom" up the road a piece.

Talking about social justice made me think about the plight of African Americans arrested for loitering and other trumped up stuff. Colored folks were just known to disappear. My Grandpa Jessie once was arrested under Alabama's public vagrancy law for being unemployed. That's how White folks got free Black labor for the industries back in those days. For more on this topic, read *Slavery By Another Name.*

Big Momma's generation worked hard and aspired to be honest people. When their children complained of being cheated by the man they taught "give an honest day's labor." The Great Migration brought the next generation of hard-working southern migrants to industrial centers. The generation came North in search of better opportunity.

Life Applications

1. What might you bring to the mix to make the teaching of history more culturally inclusive?

2. Prepare a commemorative speech for delivery at a large family gathering or special group you belong. Eulogies, Thanksgiving speeches, family reunion tributes, testimonial addresses, and dedications are examples of commemorative speeches. The fundamental purpose of a commemorative speech is to inspire the audience—to heighten their appreciation for a person, institution, or idea being praised. Although it usually presents information about its subject, a commemorative speech is different from an informative speech. The aim of a commemorative speech is to express feelings and arouse sentiments. Commemorative speeches that honor an elder, either living or deceased, are recommended. The speech should be delivered by memory preferably so to maintain as much eye contact as possible. You will employ imagery, rhythm and creativity.

Chapter Eight
Standing Watch on Freedom's Eve

Why Guard Freedom?

If there is no struggle, there is no progress.

Frederick Douglass, 1857

final call

tinsel vapor,
hallowed grounds,
specter aberration,
jubilant flight.

America prepared to commemorate the 150th anniversary of the Emancipation Proclamation when Pat Bearden, president of the Chicago-based International Sons and Daughters of Slave Ancestry (ISDSA), reached out to me about being a subject expert for a documentary. I earlier was the keynote speaker for the ISDSA Juneteenth National Freedom Day Celebration at the Du Sable Museum in Chicago. ISDSA colleagues told me "You have done the research and have all the documents. You came first to mind."

I had an idea what was involved in taping for a show about emancipation. I was a subject expert on Safe Harbor, a documentary about the Underground Railroad that aired throughout the country over national public television. Yet I felt sluggish. It was post-Christmas and the Kwanzaa holiday. Friends from various walks of life told me they caught Safe Harbor on the air. I detected a sense of urgency. So I agreed.

If there is no struggle, there is no progress.

Frederick Douglass, 1857

Well, that old Lincoln was a great, big man. He freed the colored, some folks say.

But heaps of damage already had been done. No stroke of the pen would ever remove. Slavery went on in the minds of the people, leaving a lasting stain on the nation's soul. Reckon, why heaps leftin' to do.

The African American encounter, which spans 300+ years, can be interpreted through progressing, sometimes declining, degrees of freedom. Prior to 1865 my people, who were not enslaved, lived "quasi-free," an appropriate term coined by the well-known historian John Hope Franklin author of *From Slavery to Freedom*. Following the Emancipation Proclamation race relations were slow to change, as hungry colored workers and strapped planter soon realized. Some White folks planned to keep slavery going just under a different name. Slavery was kept going under sharecropping.

For more in this topic, see the documentary *All God's Dangers*.

One thing at least for sure, the appetite for colored was not soon to subside, if the record of southern dailies were any indicator.

The Dawson Weekly Journal wrote the following.

> *Custom in civilized countries has rendered it necessary to have a class to take the place of 'hewers of wood and drawers of water'—or servants. African slavery—or the basis of natural inferiority—is the only system that ever worked harmoniously, and the only one that ever will. While the social status of the negro has been altered… his relationship to the white race, remains virtually the same… our people will embrace and act upon the idea that the negro is still to raise cotton, corn, etc. though under a different system of labor.*

Courageous conversation about the slave economic piece and residuals that take the form of silent racism got to be tackled for true progress to occur. You see, making a slave was first and foremost an economic concern. Breeding of slaves occurred. To read more on this topic visit *Birthing a Slave: Motherhood and Medicine in the Antebellum South*. As slave narratives and documents support, the bottom line was turning a profit. Granted it was a messy business for sure.

Masta Can I Fetch A Penny For My Thoughts?

Historians do not agree on the names of slave inventor, though despite restrictions brought on by slave status coupled with limited property rights they likely made contributions. Speculation that Eli Whitney's cotton gin was an advancement based on a comb-like item developed by slaves to remove the seed existed. Some credit Hezekiah, an Alabama slave, Slade, a North Carolina slave, Ebar, a Massachusetts slave, and an unknown Kentucky slave, respectively, for innovations in producing a cotton-cleaning machine, tobacco-curing process, corn broom and a hemp-brake device in the early nineteenth century. Controversy surrounded the contribution of slave inventors.

Over the centuries opponents to racial progress challenged African American intelligence as justification for denial of full citizenship rights, central to the claim was presumptive superiority of intelligence. Yet funny thing was slave masters fought leg battles to get the rights to the inventions of their so-called dumb slaves. Claims of masters for patent rights to inventions of slaves led to legal decisions and varied from the Union to Confederacy. In 1858, the U.S Attorney General Jeremiah S. Black upheld a decision made by the Secretary of Interior, which was brought to him upon appeal from the Commissioner of Patents. His decision upheld a patent was unable to be issued to a slave or prospective master, because according to the law a slave was not recognized as a U.S. citizen and was unable to enter into any binding contracts.

Jefferson Davis, President of the Confederate States of America, was unsuccessful in an attempt to patent the invention of a slave on his plantation, Benjamin T. Montgomery, African American inventor of a boat propeller. This incident led to a recommendation by President Jefferson Davis to the Congress of the Confederate States of America which passed into law that granted prospective masters a patent for the discovery and inventions of their slaves. Historians have been confronted by obscurity when searching the official USPO record for enslaved inventors, though a few legal briefs and oral accounts exist that support the descendants of enslaved Africans invented mechanical devices to ease their workload.

Making and Re-making a Slave, How Can We Break the Slave Cycle?

Slavery was kept going by sharecropping, the convict-lease system, the school-to-prison pipeline and ghettoes. Some White folks figured out ways to keep my people in debt. The police and legal system worked hand in hand to arrest folks for being unemployed or poor and to get them in the system. My people were employed by industries for basically free. For more on this topic, read *Slavery By Another Name: The Re-enslavement of Black Americans from the Civil War to World War II*.

"Why are we *reminiscing* about slavery?" A caller asked. I was invited to be a guest on a conservative talk radio show. Slavery has made many casualties, both Black and White alike, in America. I have found a fear and social uncomfortableness about discussion of slavery and race matters. America can ill afford to hide from truths that make us feel uncomfortable.

Challenge the myth that "slavery was not so bad." Believe you me, the myth is out there. In recent times I have heard it stated from some educators in some urban communities. You can see why youth of all races have expressed dismay concerning the lack of knowledge about diversity in the public schools.

Here are a few tips to challenge the myth.

- Take a tour of Whitney Plantation and Museum. You're in for a reality check. See busts of enslaved persons's heads on posts as occurred in aftermath of slave revolt during 19th century.

- Show the uninformed a photo of enslaved African Gordon's scarred back found on page 17 of Velma Maia Thomas's *Lest We Forget: The Passage from Africa to Slavery and Emancipation* (Crown Publishers 1997).

- Outline how slaves were made.

- Share the following reading list on "making a slave." For scholarly readings, see twentieth century historians Ira Berlin's *Many Thousands Gone: The First Two Centuries of Slavery in North America* (1998), Eugene Genovese's *Roll, Jordan, Roll* (1974), and Kenneth M. Stampp's *The Peculiar Institution* (Knopf 1956).

- Read and tell the story of Linda Brent or Frederick Douglass.

How Were Slaves Made?

How were slaves made? The findings are provocative. My people's enslavement developed over a span of several decades. In 1619, twenty Africans from Angola arrived off the coast of Virginia, beginning what has been a great encounter that has spanned three hundred plus years. My people's first Americans were indentured servants. By 1640 my people were being considered permanent servants and the condition inherited by offspring in Virginia.

One of the most concise definitions of a slave can be found in the 1825 *Louisiana Civil Code*:

A slave is one who is in the power of a master to whom he belongs. The master may sell him, dispose of his person, his industry, and his labor: he can do nothing, possess nothing, nor acquire anything but what must belong to the master.

Primary conditions of slavery included permanency and inheritability.

Ten Rules for Making a Slave

There is very little praiseworthy to be said on "making a slave." As earlier mentioned, surprisingly, I have heard an erroneous view expressed by some unenlightened educators in recent times. The myth is that "slavery was not so bad." I put together Ten Rules for Making a Slave for the layperson to help you in discussion of the slave making business.

- **Inflict Deep Psychological Scarring**

  Deep psychological scarring was slavery's enduring legacy. Captors desired to generate fear of quick and swift reprisals to discourage rebellion. They struck fear into the heart of my people with the tools of psychological torture, which included murder, rape, maiming, lynching, burning at the stake, and deprivation of food, clothing, and creature comforts.

  Once my people were exposed to these atrocities, the news spread like wildfire. Deep psychological scarring was the outcome, which entered into my people's family systems and was passed on. Through the informal grapevine the enslaved communities heard of these atrocities and passed the stories on.

  Enslaved ancestor's breaking in process called for beatings into a stupor, again and again. Beatings left physical scars, which were not minimal. We selected as a reminder the enslaved ancestor Gordon's scarred back to grace the cover of Jah Kente International's "Redemption Ritual Inviting the Ancestors to be Present" program held at the Frederick Douglass National Historic Site in Washington, DC on August 31, 2001. Read Solomon Northup's narrative *Twelve Years a Slave: Narrative of Solomon Northup, a Citizen of New-York, Kidnapped in Washington City in 1841, and Rescued in 1853* for a description of the breaking in process.

- **Disrupt Communication Lines**

  Slave laws in Barbados prohibited my people's playing of drums. In the American colonies slave laws were passed to restrict the use of talking drums, which provided an effective way to communicate news from one plantation to another. Restrictions upon public gatherings further limited the transmission of knowledge. My people were not permitted to speak their Mother tongue, which was being lost by the third and fourth generations except in secluded regions on the Sea Islands.

- **Forbid Learning To Read or Write**

  Our great liberator Frederick Douglass secretly taught slaves at a Sabbath School, though slave codes expressly forbid teaching slaves how to read or write. A few clever mulattoes, like Frederick, were taught by their parents, mistresses, or children. Frederick Douglass gained the basic ABC's from his master's wife, who unwittingly taught him. She later, made aware of the "wrong" of teaching slaves, attempted to frustrate his effort for more education. There were a few Sabbath schools, though nine out of ten of the African-American masses remained illiterate upon freedom.

  Captors expressed an unwillingness to instruct my people in their preferred form of communication, the written word. Read Thomas Webber's *Deep Like the Rivers: Education in the Slave Quarter Community* (W.W. Norton 1978) to learn how enslaved communities passed on knowledge and culture through storytelling, secret church meetings and other means.

- **Devalue a People's Past**

  My people had a glorious past. Ethiopians were esteemed in antiquity. Great civilizations included Mali, Ghana, Songhay, and Carthage. Libraries existed in Timbuctoo and Carthage.

  Captors devalued Africa's glorious past. They mocked my people for their earth-tone skin, thick lips, wide nostrils, kinky hair, and voluptuous behinds. My people re-identified themselves with their captor when then were stripped of their language, traditions, and culture.

- **Teach the Myth of the Captor's Superiority**

The Chesapeake Region, which included Virginia and Maryland, was a slaving center. In 1676, a show of support from enslaved Africans, who one out of ten participated in Bacon's rebellion, what was said to be an English class, signaled a warning to wealthy whites. The alarm was over the cooperation between mistreated European indentured servants and enslaved Africans in Virginia. European indentured servants were being underfed and overworked.

What was the white aristocracy to do? The planters studied the problem. A concern about European indentured complaints, getting back to their homeland, was real. However, little likelihood of complaints about slavery getting back to Africa existed. Who did enslaved Africans have to appeal for legal redress after all? Planters arrived with an answer. A greater wedge was to be drawn between whites of all classes and my people!

Wealthy planters fired back and began to place greater emphasis upon racial differences rather than class, promoting the myth of white superiority. White indentured servants, poor whites, and white females all were to feel superior to my people. The strategy was tied to a decrease in the reliance of indentured white servants and increase in the importation of Africans. A wedge was driven between poor whites and my people. The strategy effectively worked.

- **Foster an Atmosphere of Division**

The Willie Lynch speech, broadcasted at the Million Man March in 1995, probably is best known for how to make a slave. White aristocrats used a method of divide and conquer, again and again. The greatest of all strategies for diffusing unrest was to pit one slave against the other: the slaves vs. overseers; house slave vs. the field slave; dark skinned vs. mulatto; and country vs. urban.

- **Afford No Legal Protection To Marriage and The Family**

  The separation of families for my people, who were communal and family loving, was one of the greatest fears. Pauli Murray, who authored a family account *Proud Shoes* (Harper and Rowe 1956) tells how captor Sidney Smith had the power to dissolve her enslaved ancestor Harriet and free person of color Reuben Day's marriage. Lustful Smith then was at liberty to fulfill his sexual desires with her, which he did. Any marriage involving an enslaved partner, if it was between either a free person of color or another enslaved person, was afforded no legal protection. Noticeably absent from the pronouncement at all slave wedding ceremonies was "until death do you part."

- **Pass Slave Status On Through the Mother**

  Chattel or moveable property, like livestock, became the accepted slave status of my people. Lustful captors often raped my people's women. To boot, the offspring was about two hundred dollars in the captor's pouch. For an enslaved woman's perspective on these sexual advances, read Linda Brent's *Incidents in the Life of a Slave Girl* and Jean Fagan Yellin's *Harriet Jacobs: A Life*.

  In *Proud Shoes* planter Mary Ruffin Smith listed her mulatto nieces, who born to both of her brothers and an enslaved woman Harriet, on the 1860 census as chattel, also known as moveable property. The captors came to physical blows over the beautiful Harriet. Mary Smith's nieces, who remained inheritable property, were at risk of sale and the associated risk of sexual exploitation and rape when and if the Smiths died. The condition of slavery that the enslaved status of a mother was inheritable gave my people's women few avenues out. This represented an exception to British law which had held that a child followed the status of their father.

- **Reorient to Captor's World View and Interests**

  My people boasted in what their captor possessed, though captors held out few carrots. Some gave a dress or hat or an increase in the food allotment for a newborn. Others promised freedom for certain work. As Sojourner Truth found the promises were sometimes empty. She met her end of such a deal for freedom and then her captor reneged. All hope of continued enslaved family and community life as it remained centered upon the economic success of the plantation.

  My people lacked few, if any, material possessions and had a total dependence upon their captors. From the early eighteenth century up until the American Revolution, Elias Ball, a large plantation owner in South Carolina, provided token cash incentives to increase slave production. In 1740, a female slave received two pounds and fifteen shillings from tobacco grown on her personal assigned patch, though it was not enough to purchase her freedom.

- **Create the Myth of the Happy Slave**

  Captors circulated the "Myth of the Happy Slave." My people amazingly withstood such an onslaught and still have laughter. Frederick Douglass tells the story of an enslaved African, who complained about hardship—not being fed enough—and was sold away from the family. Interestingly, through laughter my people coped with the absurdity of the slave world. Laughter was a mask to release pent up emotions, take a jab at unequal status, and to reconstruct my people's fragile existence.

Slave Resistance

The first and second generations of my people generally were openly defiant. There were those who fought. Some seized slave vessels. Others committed suicide. Enslaved Africans tended to run away in small groups in hopes of establishing maroon societies in swamps and secluded beaches.

I have a signed copy of the catalog for the exhibition, "The Haitian Revolution: Celebrating the First Black Republic in America." In 1510, the first shipment of enslaved Africans was brought to Saint-Domingue, later known as Haiti. In 1522, the first major slave revolt occurred. Famous slave revolts occurred in Saint-Domingue. In 1789, the Mulattoes began the slave revolt. The Mulattoes, who were free but with few rights, were unsuccessful. This revolt was put down. But the former enslaved Black Africans continued the revolt under the leadership of Jean-Jacques Dessalines, Henri Christophe and Toussaint L'Ouverture. Finally, the French sent an army to put down the revolt. But the army succumbed to malaria. In 1799, Napoleon sent 20,000 troops and re-introduces slavery. Then the Black peasants revolted. Napoleon tricked Toussaint L'Ouverture, a brilliant tactical military leader, to come to France. In 1803, Toussaint died in French dungeon. Dessalines got the Mulattoes to join with the Blacks and they finally drove the French off of the island. Under Jean-Jacques Dessalines the country of Haiti became independent. The Haitian Revolution, a later slave revolt, established the first independent Black Republic in the America.

In Brazil the enslaved African persons revolted. In Brazil and islands enslaved Africans used the mountainous areas, primitive roads and dense jungle to their advantage. Leadership established an independent African republic which survived from 1650 to 1696. Under the military leadership of Zumbi, the Republic of Palmares had 20,000 soldiers. The Portuguese toppled the Republic around 1694.

In 1733, an Akwamu chief, King June, led enslaved African persons revolted on St. John in Virgin Islands. They liberated St. Thomas and Tortuga. St. John held out for 6 months. The enslaved Africans fought. Some committed collective ritual death in pursuit of freedom.

In United States scholars have documented about twelve slave revolts. The ratio of Whites to Blacks in the United States contributed to less slave revolts. Blacks were always outnumbered in the United States, except in places like South Carolina during the colonial era. United States developed a higher proportion of native born African Americans to first-generation Africans.

- In 1712, twenty-four enslaved persons killed nine whites and burned a building down.

- In 1740, enslaved set fires throughout the island of New York.

- In 1739, South Carolina involved 50 to 100 slaves who killed some white men and tried to march south trying to join the Native Americans. About 50 slaves were killed.

- In 1740, Stono, South Carolina another slave revolt was caught before it got off the ground.

- In 19th century the Gabriel Prosser insurrection occurred right outside of Richmond. They were going to seize the armory. Gabriel's wife was a skilled sword maker. There were 1,000 slaves involved.

- In 1810, near Louisiana there were 500 Blacks marching with cane knives in their hands. The revolt savagely was put down. As earlier mentioned, enslaved person's heads on posts occurred in aftermath of slave revolt.

- In 1822, Denmark Vesey revolt, Vesey was a free black. This revolt occurred in Charleston, South Carolina. The African Methodist Episcopal church, known today as the Emmanuel AME Church, was involved. They were betrayed.

- In 1831, Nat Turner's Insurrection in Virginia involved 50 to 75 slaves. Killed about 50 to 75 whites. Turner was a well trusted slave. Turner was an exhorter (slave minister), given to visions. In August of 1831 there was an eclipse of the sun. He said this meant it was time for the Blacks to take over the Whites. From 1830 to end of slavery there was a massive repression against Blacks. This is the period in which all free Black activities were suppressed and made illegal. Nat Turner's revolt sparked much debate about whether slavery should be continued or discontinued. In 1831, a more visible anti-slavery movement began to take form. From 1831 on there were no more documented slave revolts on record.

Beyond adversity my people framed a belief and value system. The 1890s of Jim Crow, disfranchisement through poll taxes and grandfather clauses, lynching, and the rise of the KKK ushered in what historians termed a low point in African-American history. DuBois' classic *The Souls of Black Folk* (1903) finally forecasted the problem of the twentieth century to be the "color-line." My people valiantly resisted being classified as "fungible," or replacement economic parts in American society.

Life Applications

1. What relevance, if any, does slavery have to present times?

2. How might you, with new learnings, challenge the myth "slavery was not so bad?"

Chapter Nine
Rufus Tiefing Stevenson

Cultural Evangelist, How to Invite Our Ancestors to Be Present

The influence of Rufus Tiefing Stevenson has been significant in our growth and development. He, along with the author, is an officer of JAH Kente International, Inc. He is an African Union teaching artist, who mentors youth from around the world. He presented a paper "The Rise and Work of a Cultural Evangelist" at the Third International Conference on Ethiopia and Its Biblical, Historical and Cultural Roots on Tuesday, November 10, 2015. An earlier version, entitled "A Shout Out from Rufus Stevenson: Inviting Our Ancestors to Be Present," appeared in Amistad, the literary journal of Howard University.

Reminiscence of laughter and gay times sprinkled with somber reflection on a blustery wintry day illuminate a backspace. This evening finds us at the Tiefing Collection, a cozy gallery near the Petworth Metro Station off on New Hampshire Avenue, NW, well in walking distance to Howard University.

Ancient sculptures with grass skirts stand sentinel over shelves lined with colorful African textiles that rival any museum. Here can be found a vibrant collection of authentic hand-woven textiles and artifacts, assembled in travels around the world. A mixed media of modern fabrics and designs rounds out the collection. Welcome to the gallery of Rufus Stevenson, globetrotter, Africanist and Washington, D.C. resident culture keeper.

As a child, Rufus recalled with his siblings in tow, walking barefoot across the railroad tracks each Saturday to attend segregated movie shows in town. An action-packed cowboy flick featuring stars like Roy Rogers or Wild Bill was the mainstay. He recalled a bygone era where Tarzan was the special feature.

Rufus speaks in lilting, sometimes captivating words. "Those wild, primitive Africans with spears and bones in their noses, trying to attack the Europeans with powerful guns" captivated youthful imaginations. These words might seem somewhat strange, coming from someone who someday would travel throughout Africa and make it a life mission to "nurture the cultural spirit of Africa" in our nation's capital.

He is a man of professed humble beginnings. Rufus Stevenson is the seventh son and ninth of thirteen children born to James and Mary Waters Stevenson in Newnan, a small Georgia town. According to his mother, there always was a degree of certainty about his given name at birth, but hesitancy about the year of his birth. Apparently, the midwife failed to register his birth record. Rufus notes with his characteristic wry wit: The year in question became official when he applied for his first U.S. passport while in the Peace Corps.

There are some fond memories from his childhood, he recalled. On Sundays after Newnan Chapel they reenacted Saturday's Western. Children broke off into bad and good characters and had a high, old time. They ran in, over and through the stacked lumber belonging to the sawmill adjoining their farm. During cotton picking, they jumped down into bales of picked cotton in the barn.

He sought out a life beyond sharecropping. As he grew into a young man, the reality that whatever he was to accomplish in life would be with God's blessing took form. There were times when hope of a better life was fleeting. His father's death, family's economic plight; in conjunction with the abject poverty of rural country life were stark reality.

He set a personal goal of transformation—to go to college, which he achieved through a warm affable demeanor and determination. Through special friendships cultivated with the pastor's daughter and others of means at Sunday school, he was to learn about the college trek. Throughout high school he worked and saved enough money to pay for almost three years on campus residence. Two summers under the auspices of Morehouse College, he picked tobacco in Connecticut.

College life represented a total cultural immersion. At the House, as Rufus fondly refers to Morehouse College, he confronted new challenges. Study was rigorous. A German teacher said, "Herr Stevenson, you will never learn the Deutsche (German language)." He took on to prove otherwise, which became his characteristic trademark. He found speeches by Malcolm X and other intellectuals about vital issues of the day stimulating.

Upon his graduation, he immediately joined the Peace Corps. His destination was West Africa, where he taught "maths," as the British say for mathematics, at the oldest secondary school, the Sierra Leone Grammar School in Freetown, the national capitol. It was through the Peace Corps that he received his initial exposure to Sierra Leone, Guinea, Nigeria and Ghana. At the culmination of a two-year stint, he visited Tunisia in North Africa before embarking for Europe.

Europe was new and exciting. There, he studied the German language and literature. Discussions with my European convent-trained Sierra Leone colleague led him to the Johannes Gutenberg University in Mainz, Germany. He met students from all over the world including Germans, who were quite tolerant of foreigners struggling with their language.

His return to Morehouse finally arrived, where he purposed to see his former German professor, Frau Ruppert. With personal charm, he delighted in disarming her with his mastery of German. It was a long-awaited day of reckoning.

The transition back home was not smooth. Many returning volunteers had reversed cultural shock. So much was going on. Malcolm X was killed. More disruption was to follow. He was drafted and served as a military policeman in Vietnam.

Before leaving the Army, Rufus applied for a Post Baccalaureate Ford Foundation Grant. His application was approved and for one year he studied French, nineteenth-century European history, economics and political science at Haverford College, Pennsylvania, and Kalamazoo College, Michigan. For the first time he was able to understand and put into perspective the history of Europe from the Dark Ages, Industrial Revolution, African Middle Passage and the Industrial Age.

He later joined the ranks of the Diplomatic Corps as a Foreign Service Officer in Consular and Political Affaires. His first post was Madagascar where he experienced that country's student revolution. As he traveled throughout Madagascar and other parts of East Africa, including Tanzania, Zambia, Mozambique, Uganda, Kenya and Ethiopia, his heart swelled at the lack of basic infrastructure.

From the first time he set foot on Mali soil, he knew there was something special about him being there. As the Political Officer at the U.S. Embassy, he was the drought coordinator, responsible for transporting needed grains and supplies to hard drought hit areas where the starving dying gathered. On one of these C-130 supply trips to Mauritania he happened to meet a Peace Corps volunteer who introduced him to The African Origin of Civilization by Senegalese Egyptologist, Cheikh Anta Diop. The book provided an eye opener.

Returning home to settle in the United States was like none of his previous returns, Rufus was focused upon facing the future with an authentic Tiefing (pronounced chafing) Collection of African textiles and artifacts. Throughout his years in Africa he came home each summer with small authentic gifts for friends and family. He later placed carved masks and statues in homes, on loan. The African artifacts continued to invoke discussion in his absence.

Now he was at home in the seat of world power to cultivate an appreciation of African art. Growing dreadlocks and drumming were part of the transition back home. He became a curator at the Crispus Attucks Museum and Park of the Arts and soon was giving presentations at schools in Washington, D.C. He recalled at the time upon his return to Washington, D.C., there was not one public or private African art gallery. The majority of African Americans remained caught-up in commercial voodoo thoughts of African art. That is before Stevenson came on the scene.

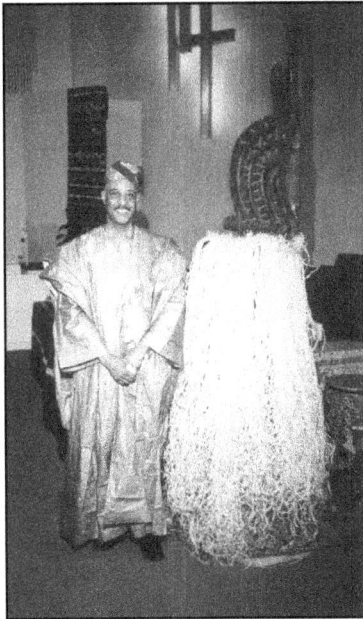

ABOVE: At Metropolitan A.M.E. Church Memorial Day Weekend recognition service Rufus Tiefing Stevenson (4th from left) stands tall with those who served in the military and foreign services; BELOW: In church Rufus Tiefing Stevenson, member of JAH Kente International, stands beside Chi Wara Headdress of Bamana people. JAH Kente has dressed churches in African textiles, brought African art to their rightful home and led an advance to return rich African symbols and images back to the community.

Over the years he has dressed Metropolitan A.M.E. Church. He has also displayed the textiles at the 19th Street Baptist Church, Union Temple Baptist Church, and the Lincoln Theater. For over a decade, he dressed the Kennedy Stage for the Spirit of Kwanzaa Celebration. As result of an invitation from Minister Louis Farrakhan, he dressed the platform at the Million Man March. Mrs. Coretta Scott King invited him to display his fabrics for the fortieth anniversary of the March on Washington at the Lincoln Memorial in 2003. He has exhibited the Collection of African fabrics in California, Georgia, and Louisiana. He has displayed his artifacts in Pennsylvania, Maryland, New York and Massachusetts. The D.C. community is fortunate Rufus Stevenson traveled to the Motherland, tasted Africa and brought some of it back for us. By his journey, our taste and cultural appreciation returned back home. The D.C. community stands richer for Mr. Stevenson's lessons in African Art history

How the European Descent Y-DNA Got In the Mix

Genealogist Karim Aldridge-Rand found DNA has also opened his eyes so wide. I earlier took him to the National Archives, provided basic research instructions and placed in his hand a sample record with his ancestors after he expressed an interest in finding out "Who am I?"

For a recent family reunion my Cousin Rufus Tiefing Stevenson had a Y-DNA performed. Tiefing is Bambara term for African man or Black man. He was a direct male line descent from our slave ancestor. What was found seemed shocking. My Africanist Cousin Tiefing, who has been mistook for being Ethiopian, had 100% European descent Y-DNA.

"How could this be possible?" You ask. Well, my cousin was puzzled and so were other family members. He asked me to explain what this meant. As a biologist, I am well aware race is more a social construct rather than a scientific reality. Each social group can mate with one another and produce viable offspring. With that said 90+ percentages of African Americans mitochondrial DNA is African, although 70 percent of African Americans males' Y-chromosome is African. That means, at least, 30% African American males have European descent Y-DNA. The findings were revealing in terms of the level of infidelity practiced among some lecherous "white" males.

Life Applications

1. How frequently do you see a positive symbol of Africa?

2. Do you or anyone you know have African art in their home?

3. What significance does Africa and African art hold in your view?

Chapter Ten
Nigerian American Alexis de Tocqueville

Kingsley Uzukwu, What Binds Us Together?

U.S. Marine veteran Kingsley Uzukwu (far left) chats with author and a student following his presentation to class.

"But what brings us together in the twenty-first century?" I wondered. "Could a love of freedom be what binds us all together as Americans?"

A modern-day Alexis de Tocqueville author of *Democracy in America*, Kingsley Uzukwu, too, causes us to re-examine what appears a common-day occurrence, freedom and what is the cost of freedom. I read his absorbing book *The Price of Freedom.* I pondered the significance of freedom and liberty, as espoused in the U.S. Constitution, and their role in supporting the ongoing struggle for freedom in closed less-enlightened societies. As Kingsley Uzukwu skillfully reminds us all, freedom comes at a cost.

Kingsley Uzukzwu, who is a Nigerian American, has crafted a work, which honors fallen soldiers and promises to be balm for some loved ones, for others an unleash of salty tears. He speaks in plain terms of how Iraqi Freedom has impacted us all to become "casualties," a term he borrows from Nigerian poet, John Pepper Clark-Bekederemo. He paints with broad strokes the tender lives of World Trade Center casualties, the uncensored lives of Marines and delicate blossoms of friendship and love. He fittingly portrays Marines as responsible leaders and salutes his Marine comrades in penning *The Price of Freedom*. He showcases the full complement/ leadership skill set, including intelligence, communication, technology, decision making and problem solving in tactical environments, possessed by Marines.

As a matter of course, I invite guest speakers that add to the enrichment of student learning to my class. Before my class Kingsley shared several poignant stories about the significance of cross-cultural understanding and advanced ground. I was struck by one story in particular of how an Iraqi risked being detained as a suspected gang member in Iraq due to the cuts on their body. The detainee told skeptical authorities the cuts were part of a medical treatment. Kingsley's explanation in some indigenous cultures medicinal treatments do include being cut and bled, led to the detainee being freed.

I must admit that on my first meeting with Kingsley I chafed at the notion there was "a class" of Americans, who served in the armed forces. I was challenged because my family belonged to the military "class." Upon reading *The Price of Freedom* I now have come to embrace with dignity and honor the role my predecessors and contemporaries have played as part of "the class" in keeping lit Lady Liberty's torch. For that insight, I am indebted to Kingsley Uzukwu, twice-deployed Marine/Veteran to Iraq. Yes, our scars have marked us as "casualties." "But, doesn't everyone serve their country?" I still wondered. "Then, if not in the military, what role do others play in advancing freedom?"

"Were we, too, casualties?" I set out to find answers. I visited Walter Reed Hospital in Washington, DC. I concluded the valiant warriors, who have safeguarded our country's freedom, along with their family members are casualties as well. Our military veterans and their families deserve our R-E-S-P-E-C-T. May God bless the U.S. military, police and fire people and their families, who guard our freedom.

Life Applications

1. Make a timeline of another culture's struggle for freedom. Visit the library and research your culture and another, other than yours. Recommended topics include the Civil Rights Movement, Trail of Tears, Manzanar, Maccabees and more. Compare and contrast the struggle.

Chapter Eleven
Struggles in Steel

How Can We Teach Our Historic Past?

I have presented along with Dr. Anthony B. Mitchell, Sr., Ed.D. Instructor in the Department of African American Studies, Penn State University Greater Allegheny, two sessions, entitled "Struggles in Steel I and II" at the Afro-American Historical and Genealogical Society National Conferences in Nashville, Tennessee and Pittsburgh, Pennsylvania. An earlier version of *"Struggles in Steel: Documenting Our Historic Past" appeared in The Journal of the Afro-American Historical and Genealogical Society, volume 30.*

A Recent United States History 101 course taught as part of an innovative dual high school/college program at an inner city school district with a predominantly African American enrollment adopted a Cultural-Sensitive Teaching Philosophy of Edutainment (a term the author coined), "combining education, entertainment and cultural enrichment" is developed to elicit critical thinking. Student learners in my introduction to United States history 101 course 1) compare and contrast historical developments, examine conflicts faced by racial, ethnic groups that shape their unique experience in the United States 2) explore how to combine the information gathered from oral histories with family elders, data from both local resources along with Ancestry.com, a digitalized international genealogical information retrieval service, to arrive with meaningful social history and 3) share the results of their research through both oral presentation and written publication.

The intro history course offered to:

- empower student learners;

- explore how to combine the information gathered from inter-views, data from both local resources along with Ancestry. Com, a digital international genealogical information retrieval service, and arrive with meaningful social history;

- expose students to original research.

The majority of students were African American, although they were from diverse backgrounds. One was first generation American with African ancestry. One was of Caucasian ancestry. Another was of mixed Native American ancestry.

Course Development

Student learners compared and contrasted historical devel-opments and examined conflicts faced by racial and ethnic groups that shaped their own unique experience in the United States. A student research assignment to conduct a taped sixty-minute interview with a family elder about the Civil Rights Era, indus-try, migration and family, using select questions from the Basic Oral History Questionnaire of the Pennsylvania Historical and Museum Commission met with favorable results. Basic guide-lines for conducting an interview found in the Basic Oral History Questionnaire of the Pennsylvania Historical and Museum Commission and Chapter 4 "Art of Interviewing," (pp. 54-68) *The African-American Family's Guide to Tracing Our Roots: Healing, Understanding & Restoring Families* were used. Persons interviewed had to live during the Civil Rights Era (1960s). Areas to be covered in interviews included all the questions listed on the Basic Oral History Questionnaire of the Pennsylvania Historical and Museum Commission for introduction, family history, residential history, career evaluations and civil rights era. Subject headings were used to identify introduction, family history, residential history and Civil Rights Era.

Student learners expressed surprise related to what they discovered about their unique heritage. One African American student interviewed her grandmother, whose surname included English and traced her roots to Georgia. Prior to the course the instructor took out a three-month subscription to Ancestry.Com, researched the local African-American community and authored *People in Search of Opportunity: The African-American Experience in Mercer County, Pennsylvania*. Research led to the 1870 United States Census of Green County, Georgia and a possible African ancestor 80-year-old Philis English. The author provided a sample print out from Ancestry.com with Philis English living in a household next door to her other English ancestors.

Course Evaluation

Course outcomes outlined in the course syllabus included:

- Demonstrate an awareness of critical thinking and the connection between causes and effects and between continuity and change;

- Exhibit knowledge of identities and American history since the Civil War, in particular as they relate to family, Pittsburgh and its environs;

- Conduct research and an oral history interview;

- Present research on America's minority communities, in particular as they relate to family, community and leadership theory;

- Write a publishable quality genealogical or historical research paper;

- Identify contributions made by people of diverse cultural and ethnic backgrounds to America, with emphasis on Pennsylvania.

Instructional materials included a sample interview between Samuel Malloy (the author's uncle) and the author. Rubrics for the oral history, oral book review and final research paper provided assessment instruments. The transcription of the oral history along with copy of the taped interview, oral book reviews, individual research assignments and final research paper were used for assessment purposes.

Student learners examined America's mosaic, grappled with its complexity and shared valuable insights. At a public forum titled "Tracing Our Roots: Celebrating Our Multiethnic Heritage" one student leader presented a paper about their genealogy, "Five Generations of an African American Family." Another student leader provided a brief overview of conflicts faced by African Americans during the Twentieth Century, titled "Struggle and Progress." The community program timed to coincide with the Black History Month Observance, co-sponsored by a local chapter of a national African American service agency, was held at the public library.

Participants demonstrated an awareness of critical thinking and empowerment. Student learners compared and contrasted historical developments and examined conflicts faced by racial and ethnic groups that shaped the unique experience of people of color in the United States. Others discussed *The Autobiography of Malcolm X* and how if you can "change the minds of the people, [you] change the world." A fundamental goal of the course—to understand the unique contribution of our own families and "take ownership of our stories", yet recognize and value the shared experiences and common threads of minority communities that bind us as people—had been achieved.

Notes

Stewart, Roma Jones. *Africans in Georgia 1870*. Chicago, IL: Homeland Publications, 1993, p. 14.

Life Applications

1. How might you respond to someone from a different race, religion, or sexual orientation moving in your neighborhood?

2. Make a timeline of some important events in your culture's struggle for freedom.

PART IV
Setting Our Communities at Liberty

Chapter Twelve
Advanced Individual Training (AIT)

Where To Go From Here?

"Where do we go from here?" At the close of an exhilarating Office of Management Services (OMS) Library Management Skills Institute One in Denver, we wondered.

"Back home, of course," came the immediate response. Unfinished work assignments and family commitments were waiting for me. It sounded simple enough. The thought prompted a mad dash for the airport.

On the airplane we reflected on what had brought me to Denver. Although we were a hard sell for leadership training, the OMS Institute swung open the doors of self-discovery. We had wondered what tangible evidence a week-long management skills institute possibly could make because, in my book, technical competence held a higher value than leadership training. In today's high pressure business world, where change is the only constant, adult learners reserve little time for nonessentials; yet we committed to go and promised our self to keep an open mind.

At the enrollment I had more than 17 years of progressively responsible leadership experience. Despite various professional pursuits, I had never received a management skills assessment. Since childhood I had approached tests with apprehension. The instruments for the Library Management Skills Institute One were less tortuous than tests taken during childhood, however. In addition, the management simulations provided a stimulating nonthreatening environment for self-evaluation. Moreover, the results shed valuable light upon my character, tendencies, and preferences. I returned home with renewed confidence.

The first week back at Pennsylvania State University, I discussed the experience with my supervisor. The report was routine, yet there was a change in my perspective. I could not put my finger on it, but I felt better when I looked in the mirror.

> *Transitions*
> From stagnation, to experiencing
> personal growth

To know thyself is the beginning of understanding. (Bartlett, 62). Before the Institute, we were a situational leader. According to Paul Hersey, a situational leader adapts "leadership behaviors to features of the situation and followers." (Hershey, 210).

My situations, which sometimes appeared bigger than life, were regulated through a selection of various decision-making styles in order to maximize the achievement of various constituents. A drawback was that our personal progress was tied to the constituents' perceived outcomes. If constituents' responses were in keeping with expected outcomes, we were an effective manager. But an unexpected outcome presented a challenge to my self-worth. At such times we fastidiously sought advice from mentors. On several occasions group problem solving showed the situations to be more complex than we even imagined.

After the Institute I aspired to become a superleader. Charles C. Manz defines a superleader as an administrator who focuses largely on developing the self-leadership abilities of constituents. During a getaway this past August, I pondered what other applications there were, if any, for the knowledge gained from the OMS Institute. I concluded that, given the complexity of today's organizational structure, the belief that the heroic manager resolves all problems was anachronistic. This thought provided the impetus to explore other leadership paradigms.

Superleadership provides a potential springboard for the promotion of steadiness within organizations. The multidimensional nature of change touches the lives of all constituents. Consequently, "self-leadership is relevant to executives, managers, and all employees—that is to everyone who works." The search for solutions requires an analysis of systems and procedures by constituents at all levels.

Why Do Mentors Make a Difference?

My thought turned to former supervisors. Among the exemplary leaders that came to mind was one outstanding library administrator, Gloria J. Reaves, at the Capitol Institute of Technology. She consistently assigned me challenging assignments in keeping with my skills and service. Gloria, like a coach, cheered for the home team. This superleader also provided ample praise along with constructive criticism and good solid advice.

When my first essay, "Stayin' A Little Ahead," was published, my mentor showered me with encouragement: "Now that you're over the first hurdle, other publications are sure to follow," she said in her quiet matter-of-fact way.

Her confidence inspired me to write additional essays. Through her mentorship I achieved in other areas. I aspired to emulate her wonderful example where I traveled.

How Can We Meet Community Needs?

I have had the distinct honor of teaching Information Literacy in Cleveland, Ohio—one of the "poorest cities in America," where students in the inner city schools have limited access to technology. Meanwhile some of their counterparts in the neighborhood suburbs each received a personal computer and had basic information literacy skills.

Consequently, some adult learners from inner city schools with large minority concentrations and limited school budgets lacked basic information literacy skills.

Information Literacy is a set of abilities requiring individuals to "recognize when information is needed and have the ability to locate, evaluate, and use effectively the needed information. There is a digital divide based upon socioeconomic factors which offers to impede future social development of economically disadvantaged whites, African Americans, Hispanics, Native Americans and the elderly.

I adopted a culturally-based approach to reach my target audience. The Information Literacy course, I developed, was research-based. The class demographics revealed majority African American and twenty-year-old and over. Majors included business, allied health and nursing. I valued the rich life experience and knowledge adult learners brought to the classroom. Recognition of the unique learning style of adult learners contributed to hands-on learning activities and fostered cooperative learning environment.

I made inroads in the workplace that benefited marginalized communities. Portfolio projects and final assessments were developed with a two-prong purpose in mind: to develop an awareness of racial health disparities and to increase knowledge of career planning and choices. Adult learners from various backgrounds developed basic information literacy skills, learned how to purchase a computer, increased awareness of diseases that "run" in their family and got on a leadership and career track.

I accepted an invitation to present on "Teaching Information Literacy to Marginalized Communities," for the Georgia Conference on Information Literacy held at the Georgia Coastal Center in Savannah, GA. Overall, the session was well attended and received, as evidenced in the evaluation summation— "The best/most worthwhile presentation I saw… well-balanced, integrated the two presenters." Evaluation ranged from "Roland Barksdale-Hall was an excellent speaker" to "professor was excellent." My concept of teaching information literacy course to first semester freshmen college-level course to graduates of inner city high schools from a marginalized community garnered recognition for best teaching methods.

How Participation in Local Chamber's Leadership Program Makes a Difference?

I enrolled in the Chamber of Commerce's Leadership Shenango to learn more about my backyard. The eclectic program offering included six sessions on economic development, education, media, environment and health and human services. Leadership Shenango afforded the opportunity to network, expanded my horizons and gave a greater appreciation of the people in my own backyard.

In my journal I reflected upon the significance of community building. While I have lived in the community for some time, Leadership Shenango provided new insights about my own backyard. The story of SEEDS, a grassroots group of concerned business leaders, who put their profits back into their backyard, reflected community pride. Penn-Northwest Development Corporation's collaboration with local financial institutions, utility companies, Sharon Mayor's Office and countless others, attracted Sunbelt Transformer here and sealed the deal. When the development team, finished processing the paperwork, there was enough paper to fill an entire filing drawer.

The insights gained inspired me to run for school board director and led to a stint as Interim Executive Director of Southwest Gardens Economic Development Corporation. Contact your local college, chamber of commerce or United Way to find out about civic learning opportunities in your community. I have been approached about service on the board of the Girl Scouts and local women's shelter.

What Goes With the Territory?

The quest for self-fulfillment has led to a new emerging self. For a few months there were moments of uncertainty as I shed vestiges of thinking that I had to be the heroic leader. I then realized that additional experiences were required for my development into a well-rounded superleader such as Gloria Reaves. Out of reflections in my journal also came the knowledge there was a developmental gap. I became determined to close that gap through further learning experiences.

I once faced a crisis being ousted from the slate of speakers at an upcoming Pennsylvania Black History Conference over my stand on the preservation of African American heritage. Risk-taking and decision-making goes with the territory. Well, I came from under a firestorm. Charles L. Blockson, former curator of the Charles L. Blockson Afro-American Collection of Temple University and Ida Belle Minnie, civil rights activist took a stand. "He is *our* historian." Their support carried weight. (Just to boot, they threatened to picket if I was removed.) I got to have my say "thanks to these exemplary elder leaders."

Let's Keep Growing

To be candid, a need existed inside me to grow beyond my leadership skill level. Few extensive leadership learning opportunities exist in my institution, as is common for academic libraries throughout the nation. Because of these observations I inquired about additional education.

As a result of the summer Office of Management Services (OMS) Library Management Skills Institute One, I enrolled in the first class of the new master's degree program in Leadership and Liberal Studies at Duquesne University. The Saturday program offered an eclectic curriculum that is designed for inquisitive administrators.

What I once understood intuitively, I am now understanding differently through acquiring the appropriate underlying theoretical constructs. Best of all, I am growing again.

As with most processes, my transformation is ongoing, yet my new sense of direction is gratifying. Thanks to the insights that I gained through attending the OMS Institute, I am on a leadership track which will help me contribute more effectively to my community. How can you get on a leadership track? You wonder.

Notes

An inscription at the Delphic Oracle. *John Bartlett, Familiar Quotations.* (Boston, MA, Little, Brown, and Co., 1980), p. 62.

Baker, Shirley K., "Leading from Below; or Risking Getting Fired," Library Administration and Management, vol. 9, no. 4, 1995, pp. 238-40.

Barksdale-Hall, Roland. "Nurturing Leadership Is Tops in Goals of Higher Education," *The Herald*, April 10, 1994.

Hershey, Paul, and Kenneth H. Blanchard. "Situational Leadership." Chapter 32 in *The Leader's Companion: Insights on Leadership Through the Ages*, edited by J. Thomas Wren. (New York: Free Press, 1995), p. 210.

Manz, Charles. "Super Leadership: Beyond the Myth of Heroic Leadership." Chapter 33 in *The Leader's Companion*, p. 216; Bass, Bernard M. "Concepts of Leadership: The Beginning." Chapter 9 in *The Leader's Companion*, pp. 50, 217.

Life Applications

1. You are invited to give a persuasive speech to an inter-generational audience of concerned citizens, who are pondering your community's future development and might consider getting involved. You will inform about a major issue and inspire the audience to get involved.

2. What combination of resources, training or skills might you need to reach your dream land?

3. Who might be good mentor(s) to help you to get to your dream land?

4. Reach out to potential mentors. In preparation for conversation practice telling your story three to five minutes:

   a. Introduce yourself.

   b. Tell, "What your dream is?"

   c. "What steps you have taken to reach your dream?

   d. What help you seek to realize your dream?

   e. Why you are worthy candidate to be a mentee?

Chapter Thirteen
Twelve Tools to Meet 21st Century Challenges

Altering the Landscape

TOOL ONE: Laugh, enjoy life and celebrate the rich African American culture

I laugh, enjoy life and celebrate life passages. During Kwanzaa we have held community book festivals. I approached African American business leaders about purchasing biographies about famous individuals in various disciplines. I asked leaders if they had any preference as to what field they wanted to purchase books. I placed a book plate with the book donor's name in the zawadi book. The book festival was successful and received press coverage. Youth received the zawadi gift books. The remainder was donated to the middle school/high school libraries in our communities.

TOOL TWO: Eat right, exercise and watch your blood pressure

Non-traditional adult learners expressed an interest in knowing why close family members became ill. I developed information literacy components with both finding a job piece and staying healthy piece to marginalized communities in one of the poorest cities in the country. To have a productive career you have to maintain a proactive, healthy life style. In recent times I teamed up with Dr. Pamela Payne Foster, a University of Alabama School of Medicine public health advocate and physician, to advance a holistic approach to health care in the African American community. We co-edited a book, *Practicing Prevention: How to be Healthy and Whole* (AHLP Communications, 2013) and organized health track panels at national conferences from Fort Worth, Texas to Cincinnati, Ohio. Working with a talented team of contributors included a clergy member, psychiatrist, nurse, and social worker we got out a holistic message. The Dr. Rev. Joyce A. Bowie Guillory is pastor-founder of Faith Temple: A House of Prayer and Healing, Atlanta, Georgia. Dr. Thaddeus P. Ulzen is chair of the Department of Psychiatry and Behavioral Medicine at the University of Alabama College of Community Health Sciences, Tuscaloosa, Alabama. Dr. Ruth H. Gordon Bradshaw is a retired mental and public health advocate, nursing educator, first director of American Nurses' Association Ethnic Minority Fellowship Program, Montgomery, Alabama. William Foster is a licensed social worker, Montgomery County Health Department, Montgomery, Alabama. Our message promotes prevention, embraces spirituality and offers to save lives.

The author teamed up with Dr. Pamela Payne Foster, licensed social worker William Foster to promote holistic health in the African American community

Mr. Barksdale-Hall and Dr. Ulzen presented together on a health-track panel in Nashville, Tennessee.

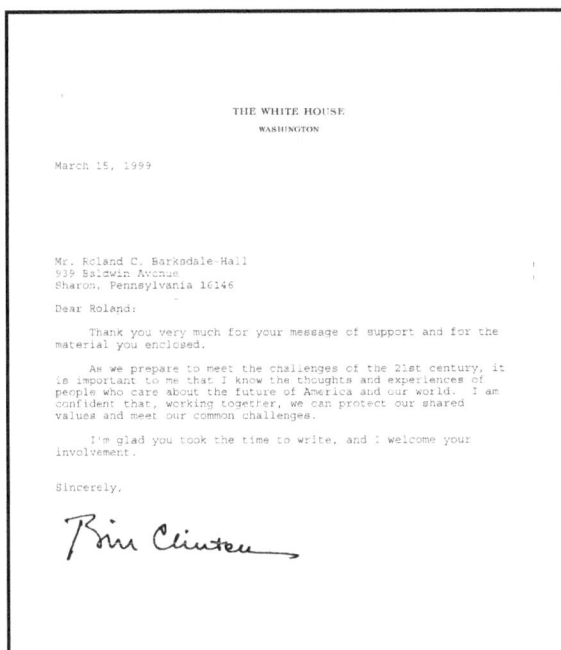

Letter from then President William Jefferson Clinton

TOOL THREE: Vote in local, state, and national elections.

Voting can make the key difference. If you are not registered to vote, please do get registered, then vote. The election of President Obama exhibits what possibilities do exist. More minorities—particularly African Americans, Hispanics, Native Americans, economically disadvantaged whites, and the elderly—are needed as elected officials. Voter ID has been employed to discourage voting by minorities and disadvantaged populations who are known to vote for a certain party. This simply is a tactic to impede advancement. Get out and vote. We are on the right course.

TOOL FOUR: Find solutions through civic engagement, partner government and community

I began working with City Hall on a community clean-up project. I found an empathetic ear in the President of City Council, who was instrumental in scheduling a meeting between the various stakeholders. I emphasized the dangers posed by the front door of a vacant building being unsecured as children go to and from school. I had done background research to know who I was talking to. I knew this would be made a higher priority item for the President of City Council, who happened to be a retired elementary school principal. There I learned home foreclosures partially contributed to the quagmire.

"How can we solve the problem?" I asked. I got involved, made the public officials aware that grassroots organizers had scheduled a community clean up as a start. It was important to take ownership of the problem and be prepared to make a contribution.

Twelve Tips for Partnering Government and Community

- Do your homework, get the facts straight and real deal in our community

- Keep an open pipeline to the media

- Know the who, what, where, when and how of city government

- Take ownership of the problem, know the history

- Project future implications

- Get on the agenda, find out how much time you have, prepare a presentation that meets the deadline

- Identify your contribution to solving the problem

- Bring all the stakeholders to the table, take notes and prepare to listen to all views

- Identify resources, tasks, deadlines and responsible parties

- Schedule a follow up meeting

- Make it your business to check up on completion of tasks and follow up with responsible parties

- Acknowledge the contributions of all parties

How to Get the Job Done?

I picked up trash on clean-up day to the angst of someone who chided. "A leader doesn't do the work, but points and tells others what to do." My rather emphatic reply was "Leaders go where the people are and do work. Let's pull together."

I maintained my work posture and got the job done. My actions spoke louder than any words. The potential benefits of the neighborhood cleanup far outweighed any sacrifice on my part as evidenced by an outpouring of much love.

Signs of progress were evident throughout the hood. Folks drove by and blew their horns and cheered our efforts. Sisters thanked us for making the sidewalks safe to walk. Friends, neighbors and family had hope once again. Children now can walk to school safely without the front doors of abandoned buildings hanging open.

Confidence had been restored. I got the two dilapidated buildings razed. Neighbors once again viewed our neighborhood in a positive light. I was commended for finding solutions. A lot of people talk, but I have a track record of getting the work done.

The Commonwealth of Pennsylvania Elm Street Project recognized the work in my backyard connecting our neighborhoods as a model. My story, "Residents, City Officials Show They Can Work Together," ran in various places.

TOOL FIVE: Read, rap with an elder and instill positive values

Wade and Cheryl Hudson, publishers of Just Us Books, have been progressive children's books publisher for over twenty-five years now. They are visible fixtures at the Harlem Book Fair. I have rapped with them about what events led up to their move.

TOOL SIX: Network and collaborate, get our dollars to work

Despite having somewhat tenuous nature and history, partnerships among majority and minority communities appear to hold prospect for progress in some communities and deems closer examination. With that purpose in mind, I surveyed approximately one hundred African American cultural institutions in Canada and the United States in order to assess levels of agreement between them and majority institutions. Majority institutions included libraries, museums, colleges, historical societies, and genealogical groups. Research data appeared in Culture Keepers II: Unity Through Diversity, Proceedings of the Second National Conference of African American Librarians, Milwaukee, Wisconsin, Sponsored by the Black Caucus of the American Library Association.

Myriad benefits of reaching an agreement between majority and minority cultural institutions have included resource sharing, expansion of community outreach and services, networking, and the attainment of goals. Community building work led to a surprising invitation. My first book was a history of the African American community. "Would you be interested in writing a history of Farrell? Yours was the first name to come to mind." A local White librarian later asked me. My first visit was to the Croatian Home. I was told to bring a copy of my earlier book, *The African Americans in Mercer County.* I did not know what awaited me. At the meeting Ann Yazvak asked me to pass around the book and said. "Roland wants to do this for everyone. Let's help him."

I made visits to the Italian Home, Slovak Home, churches with Greek, Polish, Hungarian, Italian, Romanian ethnic populations with similar results.

Networking guru George C. Fraser, CEO of FraserNet, Inc., authored the classic *Success Runs in Our Race*, which is required reading at more than fifty Historically Black Colleges and Universities (HBCUs) across the country. He promotes education, marketable skills and healthy relationships. FraserNet publishes the award-winning *Success Guide Worldwide: The Networking Guide to Black Resources* and hosts the annual PowerNetworking Conference, the African American community's largest and most popular networking event.

TOOL SEVEN: Commit to a project, hone leadership skillset and excel in what we do,

I have found the following leadership skill-set necessary to get the job done.

- Communication,
- Information Technology,
- Critical Thinking,
- Team building,
- Leadership theory and practice,
- Problem solving and decision making
- Collaboration and partnership,
- Negotiation and conflict resolution.

More than One Hundred One Ways to Lead

Live like this is the last day of your life, be a model of good character and sound judgment, organize a voter registration, volunteer with Habitat for Humanity, revisit the past and get a release from past hurts, feel good about you, jot down reflections in a journal, know who you are, volunteer with a local Veteran's organization, identify a community need and organize to meet the need, coach oratory, visit sick in hospitals, consult with a physician about an exercise plan, know your family history, research and share ethnic history of community, rap with an elder, don't tell or laugh at any racial ethnic, religious or otherwise offensive humor, serve on a museum board, focus on positive thinking, develop a circle of true friends, embrace challenges, change yourself and change the situation, volunteer at a local soup kitchen, practice conversion, know the Creator for yourself, become a mature adult, organize a drive for shoes, gloves or boots, volunteer for an assignment at work, do your best work, when asked to do a job try to live up to your word, give yourself permission to fail, learn something from past failures, prepare to soar, donate to an American Red Cross Blood Drive, vote in local, state and national elections, be a respected person, laugh at your mistakes, organize a block club of concerned citizens, promote Nguzo Saba, serve as a union rep, be comfortable with shades of gray in life, run for school boards, encourage a local veteran's family, support Blind Association, donate new Teddy Bears to a local children's hospital, develop healthy relationships with family and neighbors, volunteer to tutor youth, volunteer at local literacy council to teach someone to read, show up at City Council Meetings, serve on local boards of NAACP and Urban League, turn off the television, open a daycare, be a good parent, spend quality time with your partner, teach cooking, sewing, hygiene and life skills, be a watchful neighbor, participate in the American Cancer Drive, show what a team member is, organize a food bank and clothing drive at church, plant a tree, pool resources for a common goal, start a business, plant a vegetable garden, buy an energy saving light bulb, read newspapers and magazines to stay abreast of issues, serve as a boy scout or girl scout leader or advisor, serve on a government task force, write letters to an editor, support friends of the library, serve on the board of Planned Parenthood, plant flowers in a neighborhood, adopt a senior citizen, serve on board of local arts association, practice listening, visit an ethnic museum, organize a neighborhood clean-up, attend a school board meeting, participate in ecumenical dialogue, assist in fund-raising for United Way or Black United Fund, serve on the Board of Mental Health Association, organize a senior citizen's club, organize a field trip, begin an investment club, mentor a youth, say "thank you," participate in a writer's group, read a leadership book, attend a conference, serve on a family reunion committee, support a Little League Baseball team, serve on a Trustee Board, be class leader or Sunday School teacher, go back to school, build confidence, volunteer with cheerleaders and majorettes, throw a ball with a child, serve as a chaperone for a field trip, learn about safe sex and tell someone about the risk, serve as a coach for sports, join Toastmasters or ITC and develop public speaking skills, sense opportunity in problems, organize a neighborhood watch.

TOOL EIGHT: Join the NAACP, support the Urban League and social justice organizations

Today, I am a proud NAACP life member. On the national level I have served as a co-author with Winfried Lenders, Dr. Jerome Offord, Dr. Janet Sims-Wood, NAACP and ARL for *Brown v. the Board of Education: 50th Anniversary Bibliography* (Association of Research Libraries, 2004). I served as project leader and worked with research libraries across the county. On the local level I have served as chair for Youth Committee. I received a community service award from my Mercer County Unit NAACP.

The NAACP Legal Defense Fund continues through litigation, and public education to bring an end to racial bias in legal proceedings and the courtroom. The LDF protects voting rights and encourages full participation in the political process. The LDF advocates for increased economic fairness and promotes equal pay. The LDF recognizes the importance of education to social progress and works to remove barriers to educational opportunity. My local affiliate of the Urban League endorsed both of my community history book projects. I support the Southern Poverty Law Center, which has tracked extremism and hatred groups.

ABOVE: Michael Wright, CEO of the Shenango Valley Urban League (SVUL), Ann Yazvak, the president of the Croatian Home, and her daughter celebrated with me at a book signing at the SVUL office in Farrell, Pennsylvania; BELOW: Author with E.J. Josey, founder of BCALA following presentation, "Planning and Spatial Utilization for the Penn State Shenango Library," at the University of Pittsburgh School of Information Science.

TOOL NINE: Study genealogy and history, visit museums and rethink our past

My genealogical research has brought descendants of enslaved descendants together and led to large family reunions. We have fun, celebrate our rich family heritage and take in a cultural program to boot at each reunion. I have written two history books of the community. The book, *Farrell*, received favorable reviews for "capturing Farrell's ethnic heritage." I have spoken about the importance of preserving our material and culture, as the keynote speaker for the Midland Cemetery Preservation Association Banquet. I regularly visit historic sites and museums across the country.

TOOL TEN: Join a Black Caucus, support a Black business and technological space

I applaud the work of the Congressional Black Caucus˙ Foundation. I support the initiative of the National Black Caucus of Locally Elected Officials. I am a proud member of the Black Caucus of the American Library Association (BCALA). I have served on the executive committee and editor of the *BCALA Newsletter.* I currently serve as a member of the BCALA Services to Children and Families of African Descent. I have received mentorship, mentored others and presented at the National Conference of African American Librarians. BCALA provided a grant to promote intergenerational literacy at libraries and schools in my local community.

I met Russell Neal, Akron City Council person and progressive owner of Graffitti Printing, when I looked for a Black business to produce items for our family reunion. We later teamed up to do a conscious-raising program about Tracing Our Roots, where I presented at the Akron Public Library. Kent Payne State Farm Insurance Agency, Graffitti Print Shop & www.4myfamilyreunion. com have co-sponsored various programs. Neal is an active member of the National Black Caucus of Locally Elected Officials. We need to develop an economic base, cultivate Black ownership of franchises and support Black businesses in our community.

TOOL ELEVEN: Let's all pull together, take responsibility for ourselves and our communities

In recent times the Heinz Endowments' African American Men and Boys Task Force commissioned a study by Urban Institute and found "deep-rooted structural barriers" still exist from job application requirements to lack of networks which hinder full participation in an inclusive economy in Pittsburgh. Recommendations for change are being reviewed.

Harambee, a Kiswahili word for "Let's All Pull Together" meanwhile holds hope for spreading positive vibes in the hood. In recent times, there is a heightening edge to public conversations and an alarming escalation in violence. The role of the media in promoting machismo and militaristic types notwithstanding, we must navigate the choppy waters to safe ports where healthy dialogue is encouraged, nourished and sustained, thereby fostering better understanding. As a dynamic, cross-cultural activity, I organized an open forum concerning rap music for a NAACP youth program.

We must take responsibility for ourselves and establish personal and communal boundaries. A deep gratitude is owed the African-American woman. We need to say "no" to negative lyrics that bash sisters and besmirch their character. We understand that economic pressures propel some rappers to make use of whatever means available to escape poverty, though we need not condone the spread of harmful materials in our community. We need strategies to resist the flow of harmful materials in our community.

Street culture need not become equated with our rich African-American culture. A conscious-raising community-based program, entitled "Hip Hop: the African Roots of Contemporary Black Music" that I organized, sparked a wide-ranging intergenerational discourse about language, role models and the state of the African American community. Dialogue in and of itself is not expected to restore civility to America, though it is a first step along the road toward taking back our community.

TOOL TWELVE: Take a calculated risk, pursue our passion, birth a vision, then pass the baton, become a mentor

I served as national Youth Director for Frontier International, Inc. I mentored youth, took on field trips and developed programming. I have traveled with youth from the Maid of the Mist at Niagara Falls to Houston conventions. Youth enjoyed youth field day, where I was a group leader. We learned about canoeing, hunting and gun safety.

I was humbled to be the graduation speaker for the Pennsylvania Target Area Local Leader (T.A.L.L.) Team Graduating Class. TALL Team affords leadership training to folks from transitional neighborhoods like mine. TALL Team graduates are everyday folks just like you and me, who get involved in the betterment of our local communities. I gave the charge: "go and sow good seed." To locate mentoring opportunities in your backyard, visit Mentor at www.mentoring.org. Mentors change lives.

Notes

Adams, Sarah. "New Photo Book Captures Farrell's Ethnic Heritage." *Life & Times*, July 2012, p. 3.

"Shenango's Kwanzaa Promotes Ujima," *The Buckeye Review,* January, 5, 1996, pp. 1, 4, Nakao, Annie. "Big Corporations Have Discovered Kwanzaa Holiday," *The Herald*, December 27, 1995, pp. 1,13.

Life Applications

1. Prepare a three to five-minute informative speech about the event "What chain of events led up to the settlement of your community by various folks?"

2. What relevance, if any, does gender, race, ethnicity, sexual orientation or religion have in your community? How might you help to change the landscape and make your community more inclusive?

3. What are some societal changes in your community? How do you feel about the changes?

Problem Solving Guide

We are including a handy guide for problem solving, just in case we run into any obstacles on the way to meeting our life goals. If you do not succeed once, rethink the situation and try again.

Step 1. Identify what the problem is in three sentences or less.

Step 2. What events occurred that lead you to conclude there is a problem?

Step 3. Make timeline. Show the growth of the problem. Where did the problem begin? How did the problem develop?

Step 4. Who are the other people interested in the problem? What is their story as it relates to the problem? Are they interested in a solution to the problem? Why do they need a solution?

Step 5. What are the known facts?

—Include factors such as people, resources, costs, constraints

Step 6. What is unclear, but it would be helpful to know? It might be attitudes, relationships, hidden costs.

Step 7. Identify the best solution as you presently see it. What is the likelihood of it working?

Step. 8. Draft an outline of a plan for implementation. Look at the consequences of your plan. Identify similar situations in our past and the outcomes. Note, what additional facts, if available, would cause you to change your mind.

Step. 9. Implement the plan. Here's to Health, Wealth, and Success.

Step. 10. If the plan doesn't work the first time, reevaluate steps 1-6 and develop a new plan in steps 7, 8 & 9.

Notes

The *Problem Solving Guide* adapted from Charles H. Kepner and Benjamin Tregoe, *The New Rationale Manager*. (Princeton, Princeton Research Press, 1981), discussions and handouts from *Decision Making and Problem Solving for Leaders* (Spring 2000) by Quinn Leoni.

Chapter Fourteen
How Do We Complete Our Confidence Course?

Doing the Right Thing at the Right Time:
An Interview with Larry C. Pickett

Larry C. Pickett is Senior Staff Trainer at Highmark Blue Cross Blue Shield

An interview with a respected colleague Larry C. Pickett was scheduled at the close of a hectic workday to allow for fewer distractions. Larry, who is responsible for facilitating leadership modules and professional development courses, was well-versed in the language of leadership and seemed to have given some forethought to what we were preparing to discuss. With the office cleared of team members the leadership facilitator appeared relaxed. He now was prepared to address some key issues of emotional intelligence in the workplace. His willingness to grapple with tough emotional issues and carry the conversation to its completion, as evidenced by the two hours allotted for the leadership interview, left a clear impression.

How Do We Face a Moral Dilemma?

The leadership interview focused upon one of the toughest decisions Larry had faced as a manager at a prior company. Larry was one of only two African Americans in management, when he received a complaint about an ongoing case of sexual harassment. Jane, a white female, who reported directly to Larry, was making a verbal complaint. She reported that Robert, an African American in senior-level management, was making sexual advances towards her and she did not know what to do.

Larry was posed with a serious emotional dilemma. The problem went far beyond race and sex matters and was complex. Larry's mentor, Robert not only had steered Larry clear of adverse office politics, but was responsible for Larry's promotion to junior-level management. Consequently, Larry maintained a stake in Robert's welfare. On the other hand, as Jane's supervisor, Larry felt responsible for providing her a safe work environment. Larry recalled, "as a father of two daughters, I had to answer how would I feel if my daughters went to their manager with such an issue and he would not do anything, because it was not in his best interest?"

How to Make Right Decisions?

Larry Pickett faced a major decision. He reflected upon the decision-making process. First, he had to override a strong emotion to believe his mentor, Robert, was blameless. According to Cooper, Larry exhibited emotional literacy in "taking responsibility for his emotions." (35) Larry also acknowledged his feelings rather than "denying or minimizing" them. (35) Larry soon recognized he valued honesty and sought to uncover the truth. Larry explained, "I had to make the right decision, no matter how I felt about this personally."

There remained some uncertainty in Larry's mind about the complaint's validity and he extended his trust radius to his mentor for clarification. Larry exhibited strong emotional fitness in inquiring about the situation. Larry explained that his dissatisfaction with the situation prodded him to find the truth. Meanwhile Robert took a defensive threatening response, which indicated there were grounds for Larry's initial concern. Larry was able to bypass Robert's defensiveness. Larry made it clear his intent on processing the complaint and followed through on the outcome. Jane later filed sexual harassment charges and won her case.

According to Cooper, Larry Pickett exhibited the quality of a true professional "in doing the right thing." (40) As judged by the insights Larry shared, he exhibited strong emotional depth in standing up for what he believed. Larry showed no regret for his decision. Instead he reflected upon the situation as an important step in his ongoing personal growth and development. He was cognizant that there might have been some personal cost, but he stood by his decision. Larry spoke of the situation as an "opportunity to enter into a noble circle of individuals who have made a decision that served as a milestone for others to aspire."

Notes

Cooper, R. K. *Executive EQ: Emotional Intelligence in Leadership and Organizations*. New York, Perigree Book,1986.

Life Applications

1. Relax and chill to Michael Jackson's "Man in the Mirror." Who do you see when you look in the mirror? What message do you take from the song?

2. Have you ever been between a rock and a hard place in making a decision? What did you do or not do? What was the outcome? What might you have done to arrive with a better decision?

3. Sit down and write your legacy. What milestones are there?

4. What connectedness, if any, does your legacy show to community?

5. What defining moments, if any, would you include from your life?

6. When have you stood tall at a personal cost to help others? Tuck away what you have written in a safe place to review in the future.

Chapter Fifteen
How Do We Develop Critical Thinkers?

For Today and Tomorrow

An earlier version, titled "Developing Critical Thinker for Today and Tomorrow," appeared in Information Equality, Africa: Newsletter of the Progressive African Library and Information Activists' Group—PALIACT, no. 2. The author gave the Daniel Payne Annual Presentation on Pedagogy and Curriculum "Developing a Culturally Inclusive Curriculum for a Youth Summer Camp," for the Central Pennsylvania Consortium Second Annual Conference on African American Studies. Gettysburg College, Gettysburg, PA. He presented papers, "Developing Critical Thinkers, Today and Tomorrow," Pennsylvania Conference on Black Basic Education, at the Twenty-fifth Annual Conference, Mechanicsburg, PA; "A Community-based African American History Project," National Council for Black Studies' 19th Annual National Conference. Oakland, CA; and "The African American Community and Its Organizations," Balch Institute for Ethnic Studies Philadelphia-Pittsburgh Teachers Partnership Institute, Duquesne University, Pittsburgh, PA.

Recent unrest in France gives us all around the world pause to reflect upon what potential social chaos exists when leaders ignore the social development of youth in marginalized communities. Children of the African Diaspora, for example, have a complex social milieu to explore. Teens have responded favorably to programming modules of art appreciation with emphasis upon music, storytelling, drumming, and drawing. Giving the youth a connectedness to a cultural legacy through programming emphasis upon Kwanzaa and cultural celebrations has reaped rewards.

Violence in America is a national health problem that has reached epidemic proportions. The faces of city dwellers represent one layer of a complex problem. In my travels I have found students in a casualty of war state of mindset in urban America. A message with a reoccurring theme has been heard time and again. On one occasions I was invited as the featured poet to an urban middle school when the program had to be rescheduled due to a shooting outside. At the rescheduled poetry slam I had been invited to youth took center stage and performed. What youth had to say wanted to make me holla. I listened to a slew of melancholic poems about shootings, death, separation and dying. A grandmother seated beside me leaned over and whispered, "This is so sad." My message was dwarfed by the poetic upheavals.

Youth struggle to grow and reach greatness in a world of negativity. We have helped youth to discover latent abilities in the neighborhood, schools and on the job. We pass on the baton our elders passed on to us for generations. So many lack self-confidence. So many looked surprised when I told them about the gifts they possessed. Caregivers appeared surprised as we thanked them for sharing their gifts. They commented on my positive influence on youth.

In particular, it is critical that Black information workers not only develop quality programming for underserved youth but instill a "sense of somebodiness." On visits we enjoy an interactive call-and-response reading of *Under African Skies*. Youth frequently ask how I became a writer. I share how I created, researched and authored my picture book *Under African Skies* based upon African folktales as part of a character development series. Youth open up and share through the romps of the incorrigible character Simba the Lion. *Under African Skies* was the first book, followed by the then newly released *Lion Pride*. I developed an accompanying reader's theater and craft for *Lion Pride*.

ABOVE: Author (far left) and Ida Mary Lewis (center) participate in Mid-Atlantic Genealogy Group Executive Meeting hosted held in Pittsburgh; BELOW: (left to right) the author, then Black Special Collection librarian, children's librarian Joyce Broadus, Patricia McKissack and Frederick McKissack.

Histories and biographies were my thing. We read works by the McKissacks. They were a husband and wife team, who researched and wrote Black history and biographies. Frederick McKissack was researcher and illustrator. Patricia wrote the books. To meet the McKissacks when we were the Black Special Collection librarian at the Carnegie Library of Pittsburgh Homewood Library was the bomb!

For several years, I was then a Black librarian at the Carnegie Library of Pittsburgh participated in a school-community partnership that a cultural organization spearheaded with the Martin Luther King Elementary School in Pittsburgh. I and a librarian colleague, Ida Mary Lewis, retired head of the African American Collection at the Hillman Library of the University of Pittsburgh Library System, focused our energies upon developing a stellar voluntary enrichment program for fifth graders, known as "Self-Discovery through Heritage."

Self-Discovery through Heritage

Myriad benefits from a journey of "Self-Discovery through Heritage" emerged. J.S. Johnston, Jr. discussed critical thinking and observed, "it is generally agreed that nothing is more important to the nation's ability to meet the competitive challenge of the future than what Samuel Ehrenhalt of the Department of Labor has termed a 'flexible, adaptable labor force.'" To prepare our children to assume future leadership roles in a global society has invoked critical thinking. Our introduction to the urban classroom was memorable. Youth appeared like they were not there. Some had their heads down. Others got up and sharpened their pencils while I was talking. Yet we remember catching a flicker in some of their eyes. The teeny flicker of hope drew me back again and again. Our work was like reviving a drowning victim.

We engaged youth in discussion about the dilapidated New Granada Theater, a familiar landmark in Pittsburgh's Hill District. I researched the landmark and presented my preliminary findings, which included a photo of the cornerstone dated 1927 along with a March 12, 1927 front page story, "K. of P.'s To Erect $300,000 Temple" from the files of *The Pittsburgh Courier*. The building had been designed by L.A.S. Bellinger, a Black architect, built at a major cost by the Knights of Pythias during the 1920s, and viewed with racial pride.

My beautiful Black children came alive, as I talked about Black Underground Railroad Operators and the genealogy of buildings in our community. The children were no longer desensitized to the past. So, on a personal level, each was better equipped to answer. "Who am I?"

ABOVE: Author takes a group of Farrell students and parents on a walking tour of African American historic sites in community; BELOW: Youth present the author the Junior Frontiers International Community Service Award at the Mercer County Frontiers International Luncheon.

People In Search of Opportunity

An invitation to give a presentation for an economic develop-ment corporation provided the opportunity to establish dialogue concerning the importance of local African American history. *People In Search of Opportunity* provided the spark for a community-based history project, cited in "When Opportunity Knocks," *American Libraries*.

We identified stakeholders in the community. The focus group consisted of historians, genealogists, school teachers, Sunday school teachers and residents. Some stakeholders included school districts, local branch of the NAACP. Others were economic development corporation, local genealogical society, local Urban League affiliate, its guild and the press.

The focus group identified community needs and made the recommendations that the project be three-fold: continuing education courses, publications and a traveling exhibit. How we go back, gather information about our families and interpret it is liberational.

Training the Trainers

Today's presentation focuses upon the delivery of quality multicultural programming. I spearheaded a community-based cultural project and taught the six session adult continuing edu-cation course, which was offered with program goals: to promote tolerance and to develop critical thinking skills, when I was head librarian at the Penn State Shenango Campus. The library's empow-ering mission embraced the library as a cultural center. Doctor Debbie Dewitt, early child education specialist, analyzed "the reflective-thinking strategies that teachers use in the creation of culturally inclusive curricula." Observation of some white "teacher's inability to diagnose what teaching strategy was not working for African-American students" led to the development of a new course, "Handling Cultural Diversity in the Classroom: The Black Child." Information workers too "need information that would enable them to engage in critical thinking about cultural issues" (16).

A diverse interracial group of cultural workers enrolled in the course, which resulted on open exchange about fears and biases. Such candid moments were critical, as Dr. Dewitt has explained in fostering understanding of "cultural diversity more clearly" and increased "sensitivity to the cultural realities of others" (17). Discussion of a slave reenactment revealed that deep-seated sentiments concerning past events, moreover the African slave experience continues to exist within America.

The final session evolved into a rap session concerning race relations. We reached the moment of truth, where courageous conversations occurred. A Black merchant shared how she and her husband, a Black policeman, felt when as prospective home buyers they learned that they were not welcome in certain areas of the community. Sessions sprung the door open to truth-telling and an increase in self-awareness.

Overall student evaluations ranked the class from very good to excellent. The adult program spanning the Black experience from the early nineteenth century to the present was well received. Through slide presentations, oral accounts, primary documents, and discussion, the group leader examined freedom in its various historical contexts. By the conclusion of the program there were signs that the students were moving beyond stereotypes and other preconceived boundaries. Responses indicated that youth could benefit from similar multicultural programming. This learning experience paved the way for development of a culturally inclusive curriculum for youth.

Culturally Inclusive Curriculum for a Youth Summer Camp

Today's youth are faced with many challenges brought on by changes, including diversity, social health, and family structure (Edginton, 51). Lawrence J. Greene, the founder and executive director of the Developmental Learning Center, advocates teaching children critical thinking skills. During the last decade the educational literature shows a major interest in critical thinking (Brookfield, 379).

Consultation with graduates of the adult continuing educa-
tion course and cultural workers focused upon the examination
of the feasibility of a summer enrichment program for youth. The
focus group arrived with the following programs format: a week
long summer cultural camp on local African American history. The
primary objective of the program was to help children in grades
four through six develop critical thinking. The program also was
designed to promote responsibility skills, which included punctu-
ality, confidence, hard work, politeness, and goal setting.

Students used program materials on Black inventors, the
Underground Railroad, and family history to bring discussions to
life. The course program, which the writer developed and facili-
tated, was offered to coincide with the free lunch program at an
elementary school. Course fees were waived to encourage active
participation. Consensus provided decision-making, yet the facil-
itator maintained veto power.

Susan R. Edginton, a youth program development coordi-
nator has noted "very often, values determine the course of action
people will take and influence the way in which they direct their
energy and resources." Consequently, the introduction of values
into the camp attributed to the success of the program. Youth
formed a nation, which they named "The Nation of Black History,"
but most of their daily activities and tasks were performed in vil-
lages as in Africa, where the village was the basic building block
of communities.

Youth agreed to operate villages, which were kept small with
a maximum of eight children by consensus. There were no officers.
Youth were encouraged to argue a point, always retaining respect
for others' opposing viewpoints. Youth worked together, received
group awards, and found the good feeling of success fulfilling in
and of itself. Youth's latent abilities emerged as they experienced
a string of successes. The Village Code of Conduct included: be
polite, be a hard worker, be on time, be responsible, be clean, be
friendly, be prepared, and be a goal setter. Moreover, honor and
self-respect were integral to village life and program.

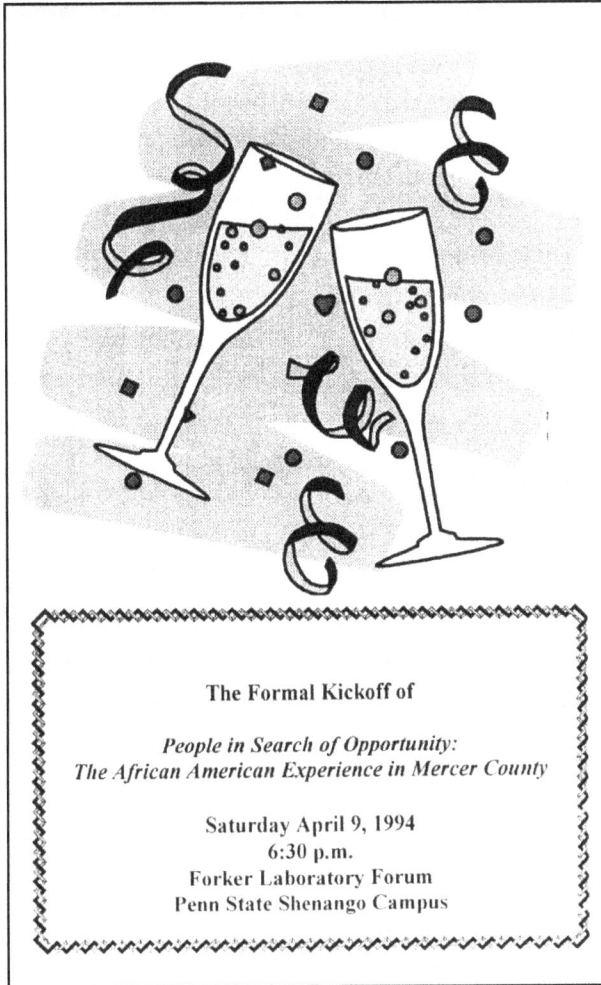

The Formal Kickoff of

People in Search of Opportunity:
The African American Experience in Mercer County

Saturday April 9, 1994
6:30 p.m.
Forker Laboratory Forum
Penn State Shenango Campus

Flyer for the kickoff program for "People in Search of Opportunity," at Penn State where author presented

Praise for Self-Discovery through Heritage

The program book for the Self-Discovery through Heritage, known as *People in Search of Opportunity*, was featured in *American Libraries*. Program evaluations of the Youth Summer Camp showed that the strong influence of peer support groups reinforced positive behavior, as evidenced in the operation and structure the community took:

"To see children from a varied background come together to set up a nation was uplifting. The children came from different home situations – some had both parents, some had guardians, some were adopted – but all worked together for the common good of their village. The cultural camp was so beautiful." A culture worker with twenty years teaching experience commented about Self-Discovery through Heritage.

"It was very impressive to me that the children participating in group learning became very mindful of their peers. They came to understand the choices that they make affected the entire group. Therefore, they weren't quick to offer suggestions before thinking about their choice." Another cultural worker observed.

The Pittsburgh Public Schools' *Reporter* (vol. 15 no. 7) earlier praised the school-community partnership. "Fifth graders at King, taught by Margaret Lewis, are proud of their multicultural project. In partnership with Lewis, Roland Barksdale-Hall, executive director, Pittsburgh Afro-American Historical and Genealogical Society, is teaching students to do genealogical research. Students also are learning the African-American history of their school community, located on Pittsburgh's North Side. Barksdale-Hall shares his expertise—and the magic of historical research—through games, activities, slides, and video presentations."

I soon was asked to share my successful ideas for multicultural programming to the Balch Institute's Philadelphia Pittsburgh Teacher Partnership. Gail F. Elliott, a Philadelphia teacher in her evaluation: *"Savored our conversation at Duquesne University, as a participant of the Balch Institute Multicultural Summer Program...pleased to meet someone who is equally serious about our youth and instilling pride in them. They indeed are our future...I would like to extend an open invitation to you to visit my school, and meet with my beloved children."*

Our children will treasure a gift of heritage forever. Don't be surprised if they show their appreciation. Finally, the children at the Martin Luther King Elementary School nominated me to be a KDKA Television New Pittsburgh Hero for my community service. And to my surprise, I was selected. A television spot about the "Self-Discovery through Heritage" program aired throughout the city. How was that for a show of appreciation?

Notes

Brookfield, Stephen D. "What It Means to Think Critically," in Chapter 49 of The Leader's Companion New York: The Free Press, 1995.

Dewitt, Debbie, "Thinking about Diversity, Some Critical Issues," National Forum, vol. 74, no. 1, winter 1994, 16-18.

Edginton, Susan R. "Promoting Positive Values," Camping Magazine, March-April 1993, 51-55.

Greene, Lawrence W. Smarter Kids Los Angles: Body Press, 1987.

Johnston, J.S., Jr. and Associates. Educating Managers: Executive Effectiveness Through Liberal Learning San Francisco: Jossey-Bass, 1980.

"Opportunity Knocks" *American Libraries*; Abston, "Building Bridges to Unity," College *and Research Libraries News* January 1995, p. 31.

Singleton, Glenn E. and Curtis Linton. *Courageous Conversations About Race: A Field Guide For Achieving Equity In Schools.* Thousand Oaks, CA: Corwin Press, 2006.

Life Applications

1. What role, if any, should community play in preparing youth for future leadership?

2. What good can you anticipate in your community?

Anticipate the good so you may enjoy it.

Ethiopian Proverb

Conclusion

How did you find your community? Sure there remains work—plenty of work—to be done. Yet I am leaving my community better than I found it. I do not expect racism, sexism, ignorance to go away. I do realize under fire we can change the world for the better though. May each one reach, may each one teach one.

Peace be unto you,
Roland Barksdale-Hall

Commitment

This is a call. The world desperately is in need of leaders who can soar.

Affirmation

Now, that I have found my roots and eagle wings, I no longer can be content to merely dream of flying. For my Creator has made me to soar and shows me. I do not soar by flapping. Yet by letting go, free falling, and turning my wings toward the wind do I soar.

Commitment

Today, I commit to get back on a leadership track to contribute to my community. As my life becomes free of noise and distractions, my load lightens, freeing me to soar higher and higher. I humble myself, turn from folly and straighten myself up and fly right.

Signed_____

Date_____

Please feel free to write and tell us about what good seed you have sown to share on my website in the works and with our readers in my future book.

Roland Barksdale-Hall, President
Barksdale-Hall Educational Services & Training
939 Baldwin Avenue, Suite 1
Sharon, PA 16146
barksdalehall@gmail.com

About the Author

Roland Barksdale-Hall currently serves as president of JAH Kente International and vice president of Black Men for Progress. He is the president of Barksdale-Hall Educational Services and Training, national youth director for Frontiers International, Inc. and author of *The African-American Family's Guide to Tracing Our Roots: Healing, Understanding & Restoring Our Families.* He is a recipient of the prestigious 2014 Afro-American Historical Society and Genealogical Society (AAHGS) James Dent Walker Award, the highest award bestowed upon a member and serves as the AAHGS Director of Publications. He is the recipient of the 2013 AAHGS Distinguished Service Award and President's Award, 2003 National History Award and served as the Peabody Librarian at Hampton University. He is a member of the 1995 Leadership Shenango, graduate class of leadership at Duquesne University and wrote a contemporary leadership column for *The Herald.* He is the founder and executive director of the Afro-American Historical and Genealogical Society of Pittsburgh, National AIDS Book Project Coordinator, founding publisher of *The Alleghenian* and *The Health Reporter* and was named a New Pittsburgh Hero by

KDKA Television. He has served as managing editor of *QBR the Black Book Review,* vice president of *The Buckeye Review,* interim executive director of Southwest Gardens Economic Development Corporation and on the executive committee of the Black Caucus of the American Library Association and on the editorial board of *Information, Society and Justice.* His family is the recipient of the 2001 Women in Ministry Shenango Valley Christian Family Award.

He is listed in Outstanding Young Men of America, Who's Who Among African Americans and has made numerous television appearances. He currently appears as an expert on a national public television series, "Safe Harbor," about the Underground Railroad. He has signed entries on "The Black Family in the Colonial Era," "Daisy Lampkin" and "Entrepreneurs" in *The Encyclopedia of African American History,* edited by Paul Finkelman (Oxford University Press, 2005) and presents at the National African American Student Leadership Conference. He is an American Society of Freedman Descendants Senior Fellow, life member of the NAACP and recipient of its 2011 Mercer County Unit James M. Matthews Community Service Award. The cultural leader has spearheaded community-based African American history projects, school-based community partnerships, "Spirit of Kawanzaa" book-fests and Freedom Day Commemorations. The minister-activist was a founder and board member of Campus Christian Outreach Ministry at the University of Pittsburgh and has a signed entry on "Inventions and Patents" in *African American Leadership: A Concise Reference Guide,* edited by Tyson D. King-Meadows (Mission Bell Media, 2015). He teaches critical thinking, literature, management, public speaking, twentieth century world history, introduction to research, U.S. history and servant leadership. He is the recipient of the prestigious 2015 Black Caucus of the American Library Association (BCALA) National Leadership Award and serves as the county's public housing authority library director at the Quinby Street Resource Center.

ORDER FORM

**Mail Checks/Money Orders to: Amber Communications Group, Inc.
1334 East Chandler Boulevard – Suite 5-D67, Phoenix, AZ 85048**

Please send _____ copy(ies) of *Leadership Under Fire* by Roland Barksdale-Hall ($15.00)

Please send _____ copy(ies) of *The Autobiography of an American Ghetto Boy* by Tony Rose ($19.95)

Please send _____ copy(ies) of *An Investigation and Study of the White People of America and Western Europe* by Tony Rose ($15.95)

Please send _____ copy(ies) of *America The Black Point of View - An Investigation and Study of the White People of America and Western Europe and The Autobiography of an American Ghetto Boy, The 1950s and 1960s* by Tony Rose ($21.95)

Please send _____ copy(ies) of *African American History in the United States of America from Africa to President Barack Obama* by Tony Rose ($17.95)

Please send _____ copy(ies) of *Obama Talks Back: Global Lessons...A Dialogue for America's Young Leaders* by Gregory J. Reed, Esq. ($19.95)

Please send _____ copy(ies) of *The African American Family's Guide to Tracing Our Roots* by Roland Barksdale Hall ($14.95)

Please send _____ copy(ies) of *African Americans and the Future of New Orleans* by Philip Hart, Ph.D. ($16.95)

Name: _____

Address: _____City:_____St:____ Zip: _____

Phone:(____) _____Email:_____

I have enclosed $_____, plus $5.00 shipping per book for a total of $_____.

For Bulk or Wholesale Rates, Call: 602-743-7211
Or email: Amberbk@aol.com
Please visit: WWW.AMBERBOOKS.COM

www.ingramcontent.com/pod-product-compliance
Lightning Source LLC
Chambersburg PA
CBHW071218090426
42736CB00014B/2872